COURAGEOUSLY PRO-LIFE

Equipping Believers to Transform Our World Student Guide

SARAH M. BOWEN

WESTBOW
PRESS®
A DIVISION OF THOMAS NELSON
& ZONDERVAN

Copyright © 2019 Sarah M. Bowen.

sarahmbowen.com * PO Box 7734 New Castle PA 16107 * 724-794-3325

Edited by Sarah McConahy. Cover design by Aaron Moore. Photo for cover by Janko Ferlič, unsplash.com.

All rights reserved. No part of this book may be used or reproduced by any means, graphic, electronic, or mechanical, including photocopying, recording, taping or by any information storage retrieval system without the written permission of the author except in the case of brief quotations embodied in critical articles and reviews.

WestBow Press books may be ordered through booksellers or by contacting:

WestBow Press
A Division of Thomas Nelson & Zondervan
1663 Liberty Drive
Bloomington, IN 47403
www.westbowpress.com
1 (866) 928-1240

Because of the dynamic nature of the Internet, any web addresses or links contained in this book may have changed since publication and may no longer be valid. The views expressed in this work are solely those of the author and do not necessarily reflect the views of the publisher, and the publisher hereby disclaims any responsibility for them.

Scripture quotations are from the ESV® Bible (The Holy Bible, English Standard Version®), copyright © 2001 by Crossway Bibles, a publishing ministry of Good News Publishers. Used by permission. All rights reserved.

ISBN: 978-1-9736-7051-3 (sc)
ISBN: 978-1-9736-7050-6 (e)

Printed in the United States of America.

WestBow Press rev. date: 11/7/2019

For my grandfather, William T. Grumbine Sr.

Your life was priceless.

Acknowledgements

How did this curriculum happen?

Let me tell you: it was *not* my idea.

I have always wanted to be in full-time pro-life work. Does that sound crazy? Maybe it was. When I was twelve, I read a book that described the horror of abortion. I knew, as soon as I was finished reading it, that God called me to be part of ending abortion. In my naiveite, I thought once people saw how awful abortion was, it would immediately be outlawed. In fact, I was worried the fight would be over before I could be a part of it!

That passion, and some of that naiveite, is still with me today.

I love to speak in churches and share the ministry I am a part of. I love hearing and answering questions. However, I began to realize that, as one person with limited time and energy, I couldn't possibly singlehandedly educate my community the way it needed to be done. So, I thought, I'll find a good resource I can recommend to churches. A curriculum, a Bible study, that would give a holistic view of abortion, euthanasia, and eugenics. Something that would encourage and inspire people to get involved and make a difference.

After some research, I realized nothing like that existed. That was when God called me to start this project. I had no idea how hard it was to write a curriculum, and if I had, I might never have even attempted it. I couldn't have done it alone, and I am incredibly grateful to everyone who walked with me, encouraged me, and wouldn't let me give up.

All credit and glory go to God. My prayer is that this will be used for His glory and honor.

Thanks to my patient and longsuffering husband, Anthony, who put up with months of books piled everywhere and my absentminded wandering around the house muttering research facts. Also, thanks to my not-so-patient little boys, Tommy, Eli, Zeke, and Jonah. Thanks for your hugs and kisses, and for mostly understanding that mommy was busy!

Thank you to my parents, Bill and Lisa Grumbine, for teaching me to love reading, writing, and speaking the truth. Thank you to my grandparents, John and Marjorie Roushey and William and Mary Grumbine, for investing so much in my life. Thank you to my sisters, Greta Charlton and Emily Theimer, for supporting me and encouraging me. I wouldn't be who I am today without my family. Thanks also to my in-laws, George and Susan Bowen, for their encouragement and help (especially babysitting and cookies).

Thank you to my friends for listening to me complain and encouraging me along the way, especially Sarah McConahy who doubled as my fearless editor, Janeen Ippolito who kicked this whole project into high gear, and Rachael Holden who is always an encouragement.

Thank you to my wonderful staff and Board of Directors. Without their encouragement and help, this would be nothing more than a "someday" plan floating around in my mind. Special thanks to Kristi Poland for her faithful editing, Mary Jo Summers for being a sounding board and a faithful encourager, Diane Double for many hours spent organizing and printing, Jeannette Bicking for organizing the bibliography, Rhiannon Welton for unflagging commitment to design, promotion, and assorted help with my meltdowns, Mickayla Nero for design help, Gordy Richards for braving the Geneva College library time and again to obtain resources and never allowing me to throw in the towel, Tom Meling for his unflagging commitment and encouragement, and Jake Habel for never letting me forget how important this is. A huge thank you to Mikayla Covington for the 11th hour energy needed to make this happen. Special thanks to Jan Booth and Bette McKim for continuously holding me and this project up in prayer.

Special thanks to Vicki Narlee for catching the vision and making publishing possible.

Thank you to First United Brethren Church in New Castle, PA for putting up with my first clumsy test run, and special thanks to Pastor David Bell for seeing the need and encouraging me to keep going. Thanks to Bethel Evangelical Presbyterian Church in Enon Valley, PA and Pastor Denny Finnegan for letting me use them as my first guinea pigs and praying faithfully for this project. Additional thanks to Portersville Presbyterian Church and Pastor Dana Opp, as well as Faith Fellowship Baptist Church and Pastor Nathaniel Wilson for testing and offering fantastic feedback.

Finally, thank you to the readers who take this material to heart and allow it to change them and, by extension, change their communities. Nobody can do this alone. We're all in it together. Thanks for stepping up, rolling up your sleeves, and getting to work.

Without all of you and many others, this would never have happened. Thank you!

CONTENTS

Acknowledgements vii
Preface xiii
Student Guide xv
     How to Use This Curriculum – Student Guide xvi
     Topics Covered xvi
     Ground Rules for this Class xviii
     Self-Assessment xix

WEEK ONE: SANCTITY OF HUMAN LIFE & BUILDING A CULTURE OF LIFE 1
     Introduction 1
     Definitions 2
     Related Scripture 2
     Quiz 5
     Related Scripture 7
     Conclusion 7
     Supplemental Scripture 8

WEEK TWO: ANCIENT HISTORY OF ABORTION 10
     Introduction 10
     Definitions 11
     Abortion in Greece & Rome 12
     Abortion in Ancient Jewish Culture 13
     Abortion in the Old Testament 14
     Abortion in the New Testament 15
     Abortion in the Early Church 16
     Conclusion 18
     Supplemental Scripture and Information 19

WEEK THREE: AMERICAN HISTORY OF ABORTION 21
     Introduction 21
     Related Scripture 22
     1600s–1850s 23
     1800s–1900s 24
     The Spiritist Movement 25
     The Church Makes a Difference 25
     1900s–1950s 27
     The 1950s–Today 28
     Roe v. Wade 29

    Conclusion 29
    Supplemental Information 30

Week Four: Abortion in My State 32
    Introduction 32
    Related Scripture 33
    National Law & History of Roe v. Wade 35
    In Your State 37
    Current Information 38
    Conclusion 38
    Supplemental Information 39

Week Five: Eugenics 42
    Introduction 42
    Definitions 43
    Related Scripture 43
    What Is Eugenics? 45
    History of Eugenics 46
    Eugenics in Action 47
    Famous Eugenicists 49
    Eugenics Today 50
    Conclusion 52
    Supplemental Scripture 52

Week Six: Euthanasia 54
    Introduction 54
    Definitions 55
    Related Scripture 56
    Wrong No Matter What 58
    What Really Happens? 58
    What's the True Motivation? 60
    Where the Argument Falls Apart 60
    Involuntary Euthanasia—Killing the Weak 61
    Who Is at Risk? 62
    How Do We Protect Ourselves and Our Families? 63
    Conclusion 64
    Supplemental Scripture 64

Week Seven: Pro-Life Apologetics, SLED 67
    Introduction 67
    Can You be a Non-Christian and be Pro-Life? Can a Christian be
    Pro-Choice? 68

    Definitions 68
    Related Scripture 69
    The Pro-Choice Argument 70
    Pro-Life With Exceptions 72
    Defending Life, SLED 73
    Conclusion 75

Week Eight: Pro-Life Apologetics, Practice 77
    Introduction 77
    Conclusion 78

Week Nine: Beyond the Debate: Discussing Tough Topics with Love 80
    Introduction 80
    Related Scripture 81
    The Tough Cases 83
    Rape and Incest 83
    Life/Health of the Mother 84
    The Case for Courage 86
    What If My Friend Wants an Abortion? 86
    Why Pro-Life/Pro-Choice? 88
    The Bottom Line 89
    Conclusion 90

Week Ten: Equipping the Next Generation: Talking to Children and Teens ... 92
    Introduction 92
    Related Scripture 92
    When Do We Start Teaching Our Children? 94
    What If My Child Gets Pregnant? 97
    What Are Our Children Up Against? 98
    My Children Are Young Adults—They Won't Listen to Me! 100
    We Don't Have Time! 100
    Conclusion 101

Week Eleven: Part One: Where Do We Go From Here?
    Individual Responsibility 103
    Introduction 103
    Related Scripture 103
    "You're Just Pro-Birth!" 106
    Discerning Our Personal Calling 108
    Group Discussion 108
    Conclusion 108

WEEK TWELVE: PART TWO: WHERE DO WE GO FROM HERE?
    CHURCH, COMMUNITY, AND NATIONAL RESPONSIBILITY **110**
        Introduction 110
        Related Scripture 110
        We the People 115
        Christians Can Change the World 115
        What Do We Do? 116
        What Is Already Happening? 117
        Group Discussion 118
        Conclusion 118

Appendix 121
Abortion Laws by State 122
Post-Abortive Healing Resources 127
Confidential Self-Assessment 128
Want to Learn More? 129
Bibliography 130
Endnotes 137

Preface

Thomas A. Glessner, J.D.
President
National Institute of Family and Life Advocates (NIFLA)

The nation was shocked when in early 2019 the state of New York passed legislation that allows for abortion on demand throughout all nine months of pregnancy—even up until the time of birth. Shortly thereafter, the state of Virginia seriously considered a law that would allow a mother to abort her child during the birthing process. Later in 2019, the state of Illinois followed with its own version of the New York law.

After the New York and Virginia actions, several strongly pro-life friends of mine expressed their dismay that such an unthinkable thing would be happening in our nation. While I was also deeply disturbed, I mentioned to my friends that, in reality, all these laws do is codify what has already been the law under the 1973 decision of *Roe v. Wade*.

When my friends expressed further shock, I repeated the very uncomfortable truth that because of *Roe*, abortion on demand through all nine months of pregnancy has been legal in America since 1973. New York simply codified this to make sure that late-term abortions remain legal in New York in the event the Supreme Court of the United States reverses *Roe* in the near future. The same is true of Illinois.

I was surprised to realize that many pro-life and Christian people were unaware of this fact. After forty-six years of abortion in America, the public remains woefully uneducated and uninformed about the tragic impact of *Roe v. Wade*.

Since 1973, more than 63 million unborn children have lost their lives from abortion. (Another fact of which many are unaware.) While the annual numbers of abortion have decreased slowly over the years (and that is good news) they are still currently estimated to be more than 900,000 per year. The first thing that must happen to dramatically reduce these numbers is to inform and educate the Christian community of the nature of abortion and the foothold it has achieved within our culture.

Cultural change on a massive scale comes, of course, through a moving of God's Spirit among His people who are then inspired and motivated to take action. Spiritual renewal and revival that will transform our nation and bring about an end to the killing of infants who reside in the womb is the ultimate answer to the national atrocity of abortion. Such a transformation, however, will come only after the people of God are informed and educated about abortion, and thus, motivated to take action.

Sarah Bowen's _Courageously Pro-Life_ is an impressive and detailed study on the tragedy of abortion. It will educate, inspire, and motivate those who read it. It is a study that should be taught in every Sunday school in every church in America. It will transform the mindset of the uninformed and, in doing so, will provide opportunities for involvement and action.

It is my sincere prayer that God will use this powerful study to convict and change the hearts of Christians in America. If this is accomplished, then we will see an abortion-free America in our lifetime.

Student Guide

Welcome! My prayer is that this curriculum will equip you to become more courageously pro-life. I believe that abortion and euthanasia are two of the most important matters facing our country today, and in order to combat them we must properly educate ourselves. Perhaps you identify as pro-life, but you don't know why, or you're not sure how to defend your position. Perhaps you're pro-choice, and you don't understand why so many Christians are ardently pro-life. The purpose of this curriculum is not to exhaustively answer any and all questions you may have, but to help you think about where you stand (and why), learn the history of these issues, and to defend, and even teach, your position.

You may have pro-choice individuals in your study group. Ask questions, and listen to the answers, but resist the temptation to engage in constant debate. Debates are rarely helpful and often harmful when it comes to learning new information. If you're pro-choice, or unsure, commit to listening and learning. Let the facts sink into your mind and heart. Don't reject a pro-life philosophy simply because you're frustrated with how it's presented.

Perhaps you or someone you know has been involved in an abortion decision. This material could be very painful. Even if this isn't something you have had to deal with, it's possible that someone else in your group has and is suffering because of it. Remember to speak gently and with love. Nobody needs your condemnation, and someone may need your help seeking forgiveness.

I hope you enjoy your journey these next several weeks. Thank you for being part of this. You won't regret it!

Changing Lives Together,

Sarah

Sarah M. Bowen

How to Use This Curriculum – Student Guide

Preparation

1. Read ahead and pray over what you're looking at. If you don't always have time to prepare, that's understandable, but try to make lack of preparation the exception and not the rule.
2. Note any questions you have, and, if you can, do your own research. It's fine to bring your questions to the group, but the best way to ensure you're getting accurate information is often to find the answers on your own.
3. Open your heart and mind to change. These are very tough topics, and it can be tempting to shut down and refuse to engage with them. Regardless of your age, history, or worldview, you can learn.
4. Have fun! These are serious topics, but there's no reason to be sad and gloomy. God gave us laughter for a reason!

Topics Covered

Week One: Sanctity of Human Life & Building a Culture of Life

This week you'll cover the basics of the sanctity of human life. What does the Bible say about human life? How did Christ interact with humans? Why should human life be protected? This will be the time to outline the curriculum and discuss how the class will operate. This is also a great week to bring in a local pro-life leader and ask them to introduce their ministry and share their needs. If they're willing, they could even teach this class.

Core Scripture: Genesis 1:26–31, Psalm 139:13, Matthew 19:13–15, John 4.

Week Two: Ancient History of Abortion

This class will cover abortion and infanticide in ancient civilizations, Jewish views on abortion and infanticide, abortion in the Old and New Testaments, and how the early church handled abortion and infanticide.

Core Scripture: Exodus 1:15–21, Exodus 21:22–23, Galatians 5:19–21, Luke 1:41.

Week Three: American History of Abortion

This class will cover abortion and infanticide in America from the early 1600s until today. Participants will learn how our country dealt with abortion and infanticide in the past and how those methods can help us now.

Core Scripture: Leviticus 18:21, Leviticus 20:2–5, 1 Kings 11:7, 2 Kings 21:1–2, 6.

Week Four: Abortion in My State

This week the class will focus on the Biblical instruction to obey the laws of our country, abortion laws in your state, and how our laws impact both the woman seeking an abortion and the pro-life individuals trying to help her.

Core Scripture: Acts 5:29–32, Romans 13:1–7, 1 Peter 2:13–17.

Week Five: Eugenics

This week will cover the history of American eugenics and its impact on modern American culture. Students will learn how God views those with disabilities and about our Christian responsibility to defend the weak.

Core Scripture: Genesis 1:28, John 9:1–3, Psalm 82:3.

Week Six: Euthanasia

This week will touch on the history of euthanasia but will primarily focus on how euthanasia affects our society today and how these effects can be countered. Finding God's strength in suffering and God's commands to protect human life will be reviewed. Euthanasia's impact on the elderly and those with disabilities will be discussed.

Core Scripture: Genesis 2:7, Exodus 20:13, Deuteronomy 30:19, 1 Corinthians 3:9–17.

Week Seven: Pro-Life Apologetics

Week seven begins the second half of the series—application. This week will cover the Biblical command to be ready to defend our faith and the SLED model for defending our pro-life beliefs. Students will be given resources to study in order to prepare them for practicing apologetics next week.

Core Scripture: Proverbs 24:11, 1 Peter 3:13–17, 2 Timothy 2:24–26.

Week Eight: Practice Apologetics

This week, students will practice what they have learned by engaging in mock debates, either one-on-one or in groups. Material from week seven should be reviewed.

Core Scripture: Review 1 Peter 3:13–17, 2 Timothy 2:24–26.

Week Nine: Beyond the Debate: Discussing Tough Topics with Love

This week the class will cover the tough topics of abortion. Pregnancy from rape and incest, pregnancies that place the life or health of the mother at risk, and adverse prenatal diagnoses will be reviewed.

Core Scripture: John 4:16–30.

Week Ten: Equipping the Next Generation: Talking to Children and Teens

This week we'll focus on how to talk to the next generation about tough topics regarding life and how to get them involved from day one. Resources for different age groups will be discussed, and parents will learn how to engage their children on this topic at any age. The class will spend time discussing what it means to parent in a Biblical fashion and how to protect our children from the distractions of the world.

Core Scripture: Proverbs 22:6, Deuteronomy 6:5–9, Philippians 4:8.

Week Eleven: Part I: Where Do We Go From Here? Individual Responsibility

This week will be the first of two lessons on personal application. Students will be asked to wrestle with tough and uncomfortable ideas while making concrete plans for putting their beliefs into action. Scripture will focus on Christ caring for individuals and our responsibility toward other believers.

Core Scripture: Luke 8:42–55, Matthew 19:13–15, Hebrews 10:24–25.

Week Twelve: Part II: Where Do We Go From Here? Church, Community, and National Responsibility

This week, students will study how God holds people accountable for national decisions and what that means for us as Americans. As with last week, the goal will be to formulate concrete steps students can take to put their pro-life beliefs into action.

Core Scripture: Jonah 4:10–11, 2 Chronicles 7:14, Matthew 6:25–33, Ephesians 6:12, John 16:33.

Ground Rules for this Class

Remember, this can be a difficult study to handle. By following these rules and encouraging others to do so, you will make this study helpful and uplifting for everyone.

1. Be kind. Many people may be silently struggling with an abortion in their past (their own or that of someone close to them). They do not need your criticism or censure. Abortion is a very sensitive and difficult topic, and it is not helpful to make statements such as, "I can't imagine what kind of person would have an abortion," or, "Women who have abortions deserve to burn in hell."
2. See rule #1.
3. Those who are pro-life, pro-choice, and those who are unsure about their stance on life should all feel welcome to attend. Questioning minds are encouraged. Let's work together to find Biblical answers and keep the arguing to a minimum. (Or nonexistent. That would be great too!)
4. Mindless debate or showing up simply to be difficult is not welcome. Nobody wants to argue the same points every week. Come to learn, listen, and engage, or don't show up.
5. No politics. Abortion has become a politically charged topic, but we want to let that go for now and focus on what really matters.
6. No wringing your hands. Yes, sometimes our society is difficult. Yes, people make bad choices. Instead, focus on solutions. Whining about "kids these days" and how "nobody takes responsibility anymore" doesn't help anyone. We're dealing with our sinful culture today, we were dealing with a sinful culture twenty years ago, and we were dealing with one 1,000 (and more) years ago. Bring a positive, solution-focused attitude to class and leave the whiny negativity at home.

Self-Assessment

Take some time to complete the *confidential* assessment in the back of this book. Do not, under any circumstances, ask anyone to share their answers with you. At the same time, do not feel obligated to share your answers with others! If you have been through an abortion or been involved in an abortion in your past, this may not be the right class for you. Prayerfully consider seeking healing resources before embarking on this type of study. You might think, "Everyone will know what I did if I back out now, how do I explain it?" Don't feel like you need to explain, just say this isn't the right time. There are healing resources listed in the appendix. Please know that no matter what your story is, Christ offers healing and forgiveness!

What if someone shares with you that they had an abortion? What do you do?

1. Love them.
2. Hug them (if appropriate).
3. Tell them God loves them and forgives them.
4. Let them talk.

5. Listen without judgment or interruption.
6. Offer them healing resources.
7. Do not condone their actions. Our temptation is to say, "You didn't know better," or, "You had a good reason." They do not need you to justify their decision—they know what they did was wrong (and they're correct, participating in an abortion is a sinful act). They do not need your false comfort or your condemnation. Affirm their desire to share. Assure them of God's love as well as your own. Offer healing resources.
8. Keep it 100% confidential. Under no circumstance are you to tell anyone what this person has told you. Not their parents, spouse, or pastor. Not your spouse. Not your best friend. Nobody. If this person chooses to share at a later date, that is up to them, not you. One exception is this: if the person shares with you that they're a minor in an abusive situation, that they're abusing someone, or that they're planning to die by suicide, you need to report the situation and get them the help they need.
9. Protect them. Do not allow anyone in your class to malign those who have had abortions. Ever. At all. Not even for a moment. Refer to the rules and shut them down.

WEEK ONE

Sanctity of Human Life & Building a Culture of Life

INTRODUCTION

Welcome to week one! Pictured on the right is an ultrasound image of a set of twins taken by a pregnancy medical center (shared with permission). The mother of these twins was planning to abort them but changed her mind after coming to the pregnancy medical center, hearing about her options, and seeing her babies' hearts beating. We begin the series with this photo for several reasons:

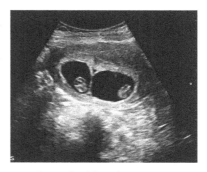

10-week-old preborn twins. Their mother was very abortion-minded, but after seeing her ultrasound she chose life!

1. It reminds us that we're fighting for people. This isn't an academic debate or a theological dispute. These are children. People who have the right to live. As you go through this series, look at this picture as often as you need to and remember why you're doing this.
2. This photo shows how vital pro-life ministries are to our community. These little guys/girls are going to have a chance to grow up and make an impact on our world because of the life-saving work of a local pregnancy medical center.
3. A picture is worth a thousand words. These little ones show us the humanity of the unborn. Even if you forget everything else, remember this picture.

Definitions

All definitions are taken from Webster's online dictionary.

Dominion - domain. Supreme authority

Sacred - worthy of religious veneration, holy, entitled to reverence and respect

Related Scripture

Genesis 1:26–31

Then God said, "Let us make man in our image, after our likeness. *And let them have dominion over the fish of the sea and over the birds of the heavens and over the livestock and over all the earth and over every creeping thing that creeps on the earth." So God created man in his own image, in the image of God he created him; male and female he created them. And God blessed them. And God said to them, "Be fruitful and multiply and fill the earth and subdue it, and have dominion over the fish of the sea and over the birds of the heavens and over every living thing that moves on the earth." And God said, "Behold, I have given you every plant yielding seed that is on the face of all the earth, and every tree with seed in its fruit. You shall have them for food. And to every beast of the earth and to every bird of the heavens and to everything that creeps on the earth, everything that has the breath of life, I have given every green plant for food." And it was so. And God saw everything that he had made, and behold, it was very good. And there was evening and there was morning, the sixth day [emphasis added].*

This passage is crucial to understanding the sanctity of human life. At the time of creation, God set man apart as something different, something special. He stamped on man's features His own image, something He did not do for any of the animals. God can see the future. Knowing full well the destruction and damage man would cause, God could have stopped after creating the animals, leaving His creation alone and enjoying the beauty of it. Yet He chose to create man, to give him dominion over His creation, both to enjoy it and to care for it.

This is the Trinity speaking: Father, Son, and Holy Spirit. Instead of making another animal, another fish, another bug, God decided to make something else. Something special that bears His image. Something so important that He breathed His own breath into him (Genesis 2:7). Not just the first man, but also the first woman and every child that descended from them. Each one bears the image of God. Not only are we given the image of God, but we are given the opportunity for a close, personal relationship with Him, something no animal has a chance for. This relationship is *so important* that God sent His only Son to die in order to preserve it. It doesn't get any more real than that.

Questions

1. In whose image is man made (Genesis 1:26)?

2. Who does the word "our" refer to at the beginning of this passage (Colossians 1:15–17; Job 33:4)?

3. What does it mean to have dominion over the earth? Why does man have the right to this dominion (Genesis 1:28)?

4. God saw everything He had made and pronounced it good. What does that mean? What is coming later that will change this (Genesis 3; Romans 5:12)?

5. God created man to have a relationship with Him and sent His only Son to die in order to repair that relationship. What does that say about your value? The value of others? How should this impact your day-to-day life (Romans 5:8; 1 Peter 1:18–19, 1 John 3:1)?

Week One: Sanctity of Human Life & Building a Culture of Life

Things to Think About

- Why do you think God created humans? Why not stop with animals and fish?
- What does it mean in Genesis 1:26 when it says we're made in God's image? How should we treat those made in God's image?
- How does this passage change how you think about others?

Psalm 139:13

For you formed my inward parts; you knitted me together in my mother's womb.

Here again we see the act of creation. God didn't wind up the clock and let it run; He is actively participating in the creation of new life, the creation of children. I love the imagery here! When I knit something, it takes time and patience. I am personally involved in every part of that project, and the outcome is something I care very much about. When my kids get into my knitting basket and unravel something, I get upset because I spent time putting it together. God knits us together before anyone else knows we exist. He sees us from day one, from the moment of our conception. Now, thanks to ultrasound technology, we can see some of it too, like those twins with their heartbeats, their arms and legs, and their little heads. Through ultrasound and other scanning technology, we can watch some of the growth process and the miracle that happens inside the mother.

One of my many knitting projects. It may not seem like much, but this bathmat is full of love and care. Nobody better unravel it!

Question

6. When you make something with your own hands, how do you feel about it? How do you think God feels about the people He has "knitted together"?

_____
_____
_____
_____

Things to Think About

- Do you knit or do other handiwork? How do you feel about your projects? How do you feel if one of them gets destroyed or damaged?
- How do you feel about God being involved in the creation of every child? About Him being involved when *you* were being formed?
- What do you think we would see if we could see what God sees during the creation and formation of an unborn child? Does an ultrasound even come close?

Quiz

We've established that we're all created in God's image and that human life is very different from animal life. Now it's time for a quiz! Look at each of the following pictures and jot down "human" or "not human" and why.

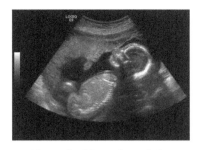

19-week-old pre-born baby.

Three-year-old boy

Toddler with Down Syndrome

WEEK ONE: SANCTITY OF HUMAN LIFE & BUILDING A CULTURE OF LIFE

The author's grandfather, and the person this work is dedicated to.

A young woman playing sports in a wheelchair.

A panda enjoying a snack.

10-week-old preborn twins.

Related Scripture

Matthew 19:13–15

Then children were brought to him that he might lay his hands on them and pray. The disciples rebuked the people, but Jesus said, "Let the little children come to me and do not hinder them, for to such belongs the kingdom of heaven." And he laid his hands on them and went away.

The focus of this portion of Scripture is Jesus's response to these children. Children at this time would not have been acknowledged by an important teacher or rabbi. The disciples had no problem shooing the mothers and their children away, and they may not have been particularly gentle! Jesus, however, called these children to Him. He touched them individually. He loved them. They were probably dirty, smelly, and squally, but He loved them anyway. He spent time, however short, with each one.

Questions

7. How were children treated differently in this time period than they would be today? How might the disciples, and perhaps even the mothers, have expected Jesus to respond (Matthew 19:13)?

8. How does Jesus's response to these children show us what our response should be to others?

Conclusion

If we want to build a culture of life, we must treat people as Christ treats them. People are messy—love them anyway. People are time-consuming—spend time with them anyway. People are always worth the time you put into them. Regardless of the outcome, or whether we believe it made a difference, it is always good to put time and energy into other people. When we value both people and life the way Christ does, we're building a culture of life. When we permit death and destruction to make our lives more convenient or profitable, we're allowing a culture of death to permeate our society.

We must internalize this truth and wrestle with it daily. We must allow the truth that humans are created in God's image to make a difference in our everyday lives.

Things to Think About

- How are children treated today? How do we feel about messy, dirty children in public places? In our churches?
- How can we love people like Christ loves them?
- How can we build a culture of life? What does it mean to build a culture of life as opposed to a culture of death?
- Why is removing someone's humanity necessary to do them harm? How does the removal of another's humanity allow oppression to flourish?
- Why does our culture value (or seem to value) animals above humans?
- Can you think of times in history where some humans were devalued and not treated as God's children? Can you think of recent events where this has happened?
- How can we bring about and foster a culture of life in our community?

Supplemental Scripture

Go to John 4 and read about the Samaritan woman. Look at how Christ treated her as opposed to how society treated her. What would a modern-day Samaritan woman look like? How should we treat these women?

Pregnancy help organizations nationwide (medical and non-medical) strive to make love their go-to response. They love the moms, the dads, the grandmas, the grandpas, and the children. They aren't just about saving babies. They're about saving society from the prevailing culture of death.

NOTES

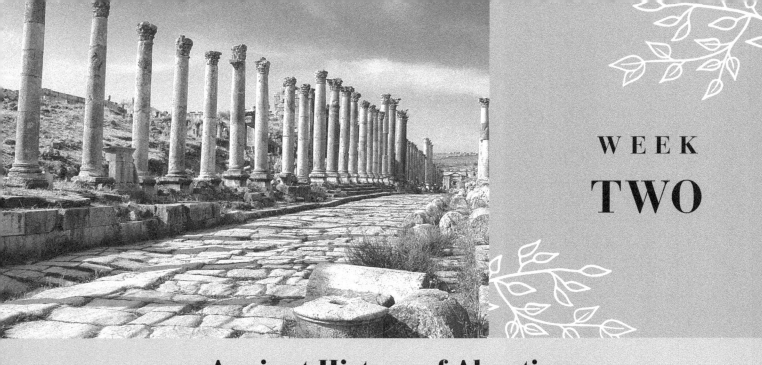

WEEK TWO

Ancient History of Abortion

INTRODUCTION

Welcome to week two! This week will be the first part of a two-part class discussing the history of abortion. Many people believe that abortion was nonexistent in ancient times and that it is a uniquely modern problem. This is simply not the case! Abortion and infanticide are sins that have plagued humanity almost since the beginning of time. This week we will look at abortion in both the Old and New Testaments as well as early historical references to abortion.

This lesson is not an exhaustive treatise on the history of abortion but a brief overview for the casual student. For the sake of time and space, we will focus on the period surrounding the birth of Christ and the early church.

A common statement among Christians is that the Bible is silent on the topic of abortion. As we learned last week, the Bible tells us that God loves the unborn. Not only that, but abortion is specifically condemned by the early church.

Some of what the ancient Romans built still stands today, let's make sure we don't include infanticide on the list!

Did all early civilizations promote abortion? Certainly not. There are several ancient cultures whose writings show that they condemned or strongly discouraged abortion and infanticide. For example:

- The Code of Hammurabi in ancient Babylon outlined punishments for harming a mother or her unborn child.[1]
- Abortion was strongly condemned in the Zoroastrian holy texts of pre-Islamic Persia and was considered equal to murder. Laws were put into place to help lessen the burden of a pregnancy or child. This society provided extra food for expectant mothers as well as maternity leave. They also prohibited prostitution (a profession that results in unplanned and unwanted pregnancies).[2]
- King Tiglath-Pilesar I of Assyria passed laws that punished women who deliberately miscarried. These laws also extended to anyone who helped a woman cause a miscarriage.[3]
- In India, Hindu culture and the Code of Manu abhorred abortion. In later Hindu tradition, abortion was seen as equal with the murder of a husband or a Brahmin (a revered teacher/priest).[4]
- The Oath of Hippocrates in ancient Greece, quoted in part below, required physicians to swear that they would not take part in abortion.[5]
- The Pythagoreans of ancient Greece opposed any type of abortion.[6]

Each of these cultures or subcultures prohibited abortion and assigned varying penalties to those who aborted their own or another's pregnancy.[7] The Persian Zoroastrian holy book specifically mentioned early abortifacients and prohibited followers from using them. They considered abortion to be murder, and it was condemned by both doctors and priests.[8]

Perhaps the most famous of these is the Oath of Hippocrates. Hippocrates strongly condemned abortion in the fourth and fifth centuries BC. The pertinent part of the Oath states:

> Neither will I administer a poison to anybody when asked to do so, nor will I suggest such a course. Similarly, I will not give to a woman a pessary [something introduced into the womb] to cause abortion.[9]

While there were many ancient civilizations that condemned abortion, there were others that turned a blind eye toward it. This topic was controversial and handled differently by different cultures, just as it is today.

Definitions

All definitions are taken from Webster's online dictionary unless otherwise noted.

Abortifacient - an agent (such as a drug) that induces abortion

Gendercide - the genocide of a specific gender group—that is, the mass killing of girls and women[10]

Infanticide - the killing of an infant

Abortion in Greece & Rome

In ancient Greek and Roman cultures, both infanticide and abortion were fairly common practices.[11] Families who believed they had too many children, mothers that did not want to be pregnant, prostitutes, and others would resort to these methods to avoid having or raising children. Even if a child was wanted, the parents could decide to expose the child (that is, leave the child in the open to die) because they were deformed or the wrong gender (a practice usually reserved for female children).[12] Not only was it common to abandon infants, in some cases it was even expected.[13] There is some belief that the *columna lactaria* in ancient Rome was used as a place to abandon unwanted infants in the hope that they would be adopted, raised by the state, or rescued by a brothel.[14]

Greek philosophers Aristotle and Plato recommended limiting families by abortion "if necessary."[15] The rich would restrict the number of their children in order to limit the number of heirs (and so mothers would not be "distorted" or endangered by childbearing), and the poor would limit theirs because they could not afford more children.[16] The casual nature of infanticide can be seen in this letter written by a husband to his expectant wife during the early Roman Empire:

> I am still in Alexandria.... I beg and plead with you to take care of our little child, and as soon as we receive wages, I will send them to you. In the meantime, if (good fortune to you!) you give birth, if it is a boy, let it live; if it is a girl, expose it.[17]

In fact, child exposure and abortion were so common in the later years of the Roman Empire that it significantly diminished the population and is believed to have contributed to the fall of Rome.[18]

Questions

1. What do you know about abortion and infanticide in ancient times? Are you surprised to find that this was an issue?

   _____
   _____
   _____
   _____

2. How does exposing a deformed or unwanted child mirror modern-day abortion practices? Does infanticide seem more horrific than abortion? Why or why not?

3. How do you think the mother receiving that letter felt? What do you think her options were? Could she refuse to expose her daughter?

4. Why would a girl be targeted? What do you know about gendercide today?

Abortion in Ancient Jewish Culture

In contrast to ancient Roman and Greek cultures, Jewish culture taught that life was sacred and valuable. In *Against Apion*, the Jewish historian Josephus writes:

> The Law orders all the offspring to be brought up, and forbids women to either cause abortion or make away with the foetus; a woman convicted of this is regarded as an infanticide, because she destroys a soul and diminishes the race.[19]

In this quote, "The Law" likely refers to the Law of Moses, specifically the commandment, "Thou shalt not kill." This quote, along with the general respect for life found in the Old Testament, shows that unborn children were protected and valued.

Question

5. Reflect for a moment on the phrase "destroys a soul and diminishes the race." What is Josephus saying here? Is he correct? Which one matters more?

Week Two: Ancient History of Abortion

Abortion in the Old Testament

Exodus 1:15–21

Then the king of Egypt said to the Hebrew midwives, one of whom was named Shiphrah and the other Puah, "When you serve as midwife to the Hebrew women and see them on the birthstool, if it is a son, you shall kill him, but if it is a daughter, she shall live." But the midwives feared God and did not do as the king of Egypt commanded them, but let the male children live. So the king of Egypt called the midwives and said to them, "Why have you done this, and let the male children live?" The midwives said to Pharaoh, "Because the Hebrew women are not like the Egyptian women, for they are vigorous and give birth before the midwife comes to them." So God dealt well with the midwives. And the people multiplied and grew very strong. And because the midwives feared God, he gave them families.

The midwives protected the newborn Hebrew babies, refusing to kill them as they had been commanded. Because of their acts of heroism, God blessed them. This was a very risky act. Pharaoh had complete power over them. There would have been nowhere to hide and no one to appeal to for protection. They valued the lives of the Hebrew children so highly that they were willing to risk their own lives, and possibly the lives of their families, to protect them.

Questions

6. Why do you think Pharaoh wanted to kill the male children? What do you think he was afraid of (Exodus 1:9–10)?

7. What could Pharaoh have done to the midwives and their extended families if he had discovered their disobedience?

8. How is God's approval of the midwives' actions shown here (Exodus 1:21)?

Exodus 21:22–23

When men strive together and hit a pregnant woman, so that her children come out, but there is no harm, the one who hit her shall surely be fined, as the woman's husband shall impose on him, and he shall pay as the judges determine. But if there is harm, then you shall pay life for life.

Here, the unborn child is referred to as just that—a child. Not a piece of tissue. It also specifically states that if there was harm (i.e. not just an early delivery), this was a "life for life" situation. If an unborn child was killed, the murderer's life was taken in recompense. The unborn child's life was considered equal to that of an adult male.

Questions

9. Do we have laws like this today? How is this type of morality seen (or not) in our society?

___

10. Some commentators believe that the life of the unborn child is not what was at stake in this passage, just the life of the mother. The punishment was a fine, as long as the mother was not killed. What do you think?

___

ABORTION IN THE NEW TESTAMENT

Often people will assert that the New Testament is silent regarding abortion. This is simply not true.

Galatians 5:19–21

*Now the works of the flesh are evident: sexual immorality, impurity, sensuality, idolatry, **sorcery**, enmity, strife, jealousy, fits of anger, rivalries, dissensions, divisions, envy, drunkenness, orgies, and things like these. I warn you, as I warned you before, that those who do such things will not inherit the kingdom of God [emphasis added].*

In this list of grievous sins is the Greek word *pharmakeia*, which is translated in the English Standard Version of the Bible as "sorcery." Many scholars believe that abortion is included in the definition of *pharmakeia* and could perhaps be the primary meaning of the word.[20] This is especially important to note when considering that it is listed with sins such as fornication and adultery. Furthermore, in the text *Gynecology* by the Greek physician Soranos, the word *pharmakeia* refers specifically to abortifacients.[21]

Question

11. Find another list in the Bible that includes the word "witchcraft" or "sorcery." Do you believe that the word "abortion" could be included in the definition of these words?

   _____
   _____
   _____
   _____

Luke 1:41

And when Elizabeth heard the greeting of Mary, the baby leaped in her womb. And Elizabeth was filled with the Holy Spirit.

John the Baptist leaped in his mother's womb when his mother encountered Mary, who was carrying the Christ Child.

Question

12. How does John the Baptist's response to the Christ Child in Luke 1:41 show the humanity of the unborn?

   _____
   _____
   _____
   _____

Also, as discussed last week in Matthew 19:13–15, Christ himself showed how much He valued children when He blessed those brought to Him. His care for these children would certainly extend to them before they were born.

Abortion in the Early Church

The teachings of the early church give us a great deal of insight into how we should behave as Christians today. Many early Christian publications condemned abortion. *The Didache* (meaning, "the Teaching") is an anonymously written early Christian document. It speaks of the Way of Life and says, "…you shall not murder a child by abortion nor commit infanticide."[22] Also, *The Epistle of Barnabas*, a letter defending the Christian faith, says, "You shall not abort a child nor, again, commit infanticide."[23]

Apologists Athenagoras (mid to late second century AD) and Tertullian (late second century AD) defended the Christian faith against charges such as cannibalism and immorality by stating that Christians are not even permitted to destroy a child in the womb.[24] Their assertions show that this was a common teaching in the early Christian church, very different from the secular or pagan culture of the day.

Moving along to the third, fourth, and fifth centuries, Lactantius (AD 250–325) in *Epitome of the Divine Institutes* writes, "It will not be permitted us … to put to death or expose an infant."[25] This quote shows that the church's horror of infanticide continued into the third and fourth centuries. Augustine (AD 354–430) believed that later abortions (on a "formed fetus") were somehow worse than an early abortion (on an "unformed fetus") but generally condemned the practice of abortion altogether, not only because he believed the purpose of marriage was to create children, but also because he believed that life should be valued.[26] John Chrysostom, in the late fourth and early fifth centuries, strongly condemned abortion and refers to it as murder.[27] These records show us that the early church condemned abortion and valued life, an example we should take to heart today.

Were there exceptions? Yes, in some cases abortion may have been permitted to save the mother. However, it would not have been considered an appropriate way to deal with an inconvenient pregnancy. Also, realize that an abortion to save the life of the mother would likely only have been performed after days of long and arduous labor. Without our modern technology, midwives would have no choice but to remove a child in pieces once it became apparent that he or she couldn't safely pass through the birth canal.[28]

So what were early Christians actually doing to help children and their families? From the early days of Christianity, we see believers working to care for the poor among them (James 1:27). They also cared for exposed infants by providing safe places to leave them, adopting them into their own homes, and later building orphanages. By AD 311, Constantine began enacting laws to discourage infant exposure with his successor declaring infanticide a capital offense.[29]

Questions

13. Why should the opinions of the early church affect us today?

_____
_____
_____
_____

14. How was the early church dealing with some of the same challenges we face today? Would it have been simpler to go along with the culture? Are we tempted to do that today?

_____
_____
_____
_____

Conclusion

Human life was considered sacred throughout the Old Testament and in early Jewish culture. The Jewish and Christian faiths have long stood counter to popular culture in their stances on abortion and infanticide. As we learned last week, human life is sacred to God and we must treat it as such whether or not the culture around us agrees. Using both historical and Biblical record, we can show that respect for human life is (and has been) an important tenet of the Christian faith.

What Did We Skip?

This chapter skips a great deal of world history. There is much more to be learned about this topic by reading and researching. If you would like to learn more about the history of abortion and Christianity, check out the sources used for this curriculum. They provide more information than what can be covered here.

Things to Think About

- Throughout the Bible and church history, abortion and infanticide have been condemned, and the church has stood against common culture and valued human life. How does this apply to us today?
- In Exodus 1:15–21, why did Pharaoh expect the Israelite midwives to obey his instructions? Do you think he would have been surprised to find out that the women valued the Hebrew children?
- What does John the Baptist's fetal response recorded in Luke 1:41 mean for children in the womb today? How can his response to the humanity of the Christ Child help us protect preborn children in our day?

Supplemental Scripture and Information

Jeremiah 1:5

Before I formed you in the womb I knew you, and before you were born I consecrated you; I appointed you a prophet to the nations.

God shows us that He is intimately involved in people's lives before they're born. They're real people to Him, not just lumps of flesh or parasites, and their souls begin long before they're born. This passage tells us that God knows the unborn and has chosen a life for them. Some people don't believe that each person has a purpose, but Jeremiah 1:5 shows us that God appointed Jeremiah before his birth. If He did this for Jeremiah, it is reasonable to believe that He has a purpose for each of us.

NOTES

WEEK THREE

American History of Abortion

INTRODUCTION

Many people believe that abortion was nonexistent or always illegal in the United States until the *Roe v. Wade* decision. In this lesson, we'll see that abortion has been a problem in our country since before the Revolutionary War. I encourage both you and your students to study this topic more at your leisure. For the sake of time and space, we will skim the history of abortion in America, focusing on key times and how they affect us today.

Throughout history, Christians have made a difference. We should study what they did and learn from them. If Christians successfully pushed back against abortion in the past, we should emulate their efforts today.

Question

1. What do you know about the history of abortion in America? When do you think it began to be a problem?

   _____
   _____
   _____
   _____

Week Three: American History of Abortion

Related Scripture

Leviticus 18:21

You shall not give any of your children to offer them to Molech, and so profane the name of your God: I am the Lord.

Leviticus 20:2–5

Say to the people of Israel, any one of the people of Israel or of the strangers who sojourn in Israel who gives any of his children to Molech shall surely be put to death. The people of the land shall stone him with stones. I myself will set my face against that man and will cut him off from among his people, because he has given one of his children to Molech, to make my sanctuary unclean and to profane my holy name. And if the people of the land do at all close their eyes to that man when he gives one of his children to Molech, and do not put him to death, then I will set my face against that man and against his clan and will cut them off from among their people, him and all who follow him in whoring after Molech.

An artist's rendition of what an idol of Molech may have looked like.

Questions

2. Go online and research Molech. What did worshiping him entail? How did this affect the Israelites (Deuteronomy 12:31; 2 Kings 16:3)?

3. God has some serious things to say to His children (and even to strangers residing with them!) when it comes to worshiping Molech. Why was God so serious about idol worship (Exodus 20:3–6; Leviticus 26:30; 1 Kings 16:13)?

History of Abortion in America

1600s–1850s

It's hard to say how common abortion was in early American history, but we know it was very much frowned upon. Abortion was a felony, and women or men convicted of infanticide were executed.[30] Based on legal notes from that time, we know that most of the women who procured an abortion or murdered their infants were unmarried, and many claimed they had been raped or coerced into having sex. While some mothers would find themselves pregnant before marriage, it seems that a hasty marriage, not abortion, was the common solution.[31] Women who chose to abort were relying on a risky surgical procedure and/or herbs, both of which could have devastating consequences for both mother and child.[32]

In early America (before and shortly after the Revolutionary War), women who gave birth out of wedlock were entitled to child support until the child was old enough to be apprenticed.[33] Who paid the child support? At the time, it was believed that a woman in labor could not lie. To determine the identity of the baby's father, an unwed mother would be questioned during delivery and her testimony accepted as fact.[34]

It doesn't seem that either the mother or her children were treated poorly by the community, even if the mother remained single.[35] Why? Because of the strong Christian beliefs of the early settlers. They believed human life was sacred and should be protected.[36] They knew the value of marriage, chastity, and community, and their way of protecting unmarried young women and their unborn children was to insist that marriages take place. If a marriage was impossible or unwanted, the father of the child still had to take financial responsibility. Until the early nineteenth century, most of the women convicted of abortion or infanticide turned to abortion because they were alone and without help. Throughout history, women facing unplanned pregnancies have needed love and support. Time hasn't changed that fact.

Questions

4. How did early child support laws help prevent abortion and infanticide? Were you surprised to discover that in early America a single mother could receive child support?

_____
_____
_____
_____

Week Three: American History of Abortion

5. How does social pressure prevent abortion? Would a young man have been willing to abandon a pregnant girlfriend if their families and communities were pushing for marriage? How could this social pressure help and harm young women?

___

___

___

___

1800s–1900s

By the early 1800s, America was changing. The country was growing, and women began to seek employment outside the home (often as servants in other homes). At the same time, the nation saw an increase in out-of-wedlock pregnancies.[37] Why? Women supported by family could demand a marriage, but a female servant on her own and away from her home could be seduced and easily abandoned.

Additionally, prostitution, a profession that could require an abortion as often as once every three months, was increasing.[38] The courts were no longer expecting men who fathered children with unwed mothers to provide for them as they did in the 1600–1700s.[39] Powerful men would often use abortionists to help cover up their crimes and prevent the mother from seeking reparations or justice.[40] As women became more desperate, abortion became more available and easier to access.

The states responded to this change in social norms. While there were many laws against infanticide and the concealment of a newborn's death, it wasn't until 1821 that the first state, Connecticut, made a law specific to abortion. Connecticut's legislators made abortion illegal after "quickening" (first felt movements of the baby), and enforcement of this law was primarily focused on the abortionist, not the mother.[41] This began a wave of laws restricting or outlawing abortion in various states.[42]

By the 1850s, medical professionals were noting that abortion was no longer unique to unmarried women.[43] Abortion had become a business, and abortionists would even advertise in local papers (sometimes discreetly and other times openly).[44]

Question

6. How do abortion and prostitution interact? What can we as Christians do to help women who work (willingly or otherwise) as prostitutes? How is it difficult to reach this population?

___

___

___

___

The Spiritist Movement

This young lady was neglected and ended up in foster care. Eventually, she was adopted, became a Christian, and now plans to be a missionary. Should she have been aborted? Absolutely not. Her life, even though it has been tough, is valuable.

Along with the rise in prostitution, we see the advent of the Spiritist movement which encouraged free love and the ending of unwanted pregnancies.[45] In 1854, Mary Grove Nichols, an abortionist and gynecologist, advocated abortion as a better alternative for some children than birth. She wrote, "The hereditary evils to children born in a sensual and unloving marriage are everywhere visible ... sickness, suffering, weakness, imbecility, or outrageous crime."[46] We see this attitude today as well. It is a common belief that many children are better off aborted than alive.

Question

7. Have you ever heard someone say that some children are better off aborted than alive? Do you agree? Why is the thought of unwanted children ending up in foster care or living on welfare something that makes us so uncomfortable?

_____
_____
_____
_____

The Church Makes a Difference

During the mid to late 1800s, Christian doctors began advocating for stronger abortion laws to protect the mother as well as the baby.[47] Throughout the Civil War and its aftermath, pastors strongly denounced abortion as murder, sometimes comparing it to the worship of Molech in the Old Testament. Bishop Arthur Coxe wrote in 1869 about "the blood guiltiness of ante-natal infanticide" and stated, "The world itself has begun to be horrified by the practical results of the sacrifices to Molech which defile our land."[48]

During the early to mid 1800s, pro-life individuals, churches, and other groups referred to abortion as "the evil of the age." Evangelicals, during the Second Great Awakening (1790–1820), preached that a separate, distinct, and precious life came into existence at the moment of conception.[49]

As early as the 1830s, Christians moved from simply helping orphans and widows in need to working with young women at risk of making poor choices. They helped them avoid seduction and prostitution (and therefore pregnancy) by providing them with support and safe places to live.[50]

By the late 1800s and early 1900s, organizations such as the YWCA and local Immigrants Protective Leagues met young women at docks and railway stations to provide help and protection the moment they arrived in a city.[51] These Christians prevented abortions by preventing seductions, and they educated young women about the risks of being lured into a life of prostitution.

The entrance to a Florence Crittenton home in South Carolina

While prevention was important, believers didn't stop there. When an unplanned pregnancy occurred, there was help for those who sought it. The Erring Women's Refuge and the Florence Crittenton homes are two examples of Christian maternity homes designed to help young women facing unplanned pregnancies.[52] Just as the pregnancy help movement does today, these organizations would reach out to women in need, help them find safety, and help them deliver their babies. This is Christianity in action! In 1884, a worker from the Penitent Female's Refuge eloquently stated, "Each of these changed lives too, it is to be remembered, is a centre of influence. Who can estimate how far and wide may extend the purifying influence of one redeemed life?"[53]

Questions

8. Individuals across the nation worked diligently to provide homes, training, and the good news of the gospel to pregnant and at-risk women.[54] How did these people share Christ's love? What problems were they addressing?

9. Are we, as Christians, doing this today? How are you and your church involved in missions such as these?

1900s–1950s

The Body of Christ, the Church, can make a difference.

By the turn of the century, abortion was in decline. This was partly due to the contraceptive movement but also to the response of the Christian community. The efforts of the Church were successful! Abortion was on the rise, and the body of Christ acted. As it is today, though, sin was rampant, and the problem of unwanted pregnancies continued. One physician who was particularly active in the fight against abortion, Dr. Holmes, wrote in 1910, "It is not possible to get twelve men together without at least one of them being personally responsible for the downfall of a girl, or at least interested in getting her out of her difficulty [a euphemism for seeking an abortion]."[55]

Throughout the 1920s and 1930s, religious maternity homes came under attack by secular professionals who tried to push them into offering material help without the spiritual component, denigrating the volunteers that worked in the homes.[56] The morality of the 1920s glamorized blatant sin and encouraged people to make their own personal decisions. This was referred to as "progressive compassion." Judge Ben Lindsey, in response to a minister who accused him of promoting paganism, said, "What I say to these young people is this: you are free agents … The judge that must judge you is your own heart and conscience … Nobody can stop you, and I for one, wouldn't stop you even if I could."[57]

By the 1940s, doctors were beginning to sympathize with abortionists whereas before they had been more or less united against the practice of abortion.[58] This is about the time the general public began to accept abortion as a necessary solution for young women with an unplanned pregnancy. This acceptance is partly due to the work of the eugenics movement of the 1920s and 1930s. (More on that in week five.)

By the 1950s, the press was differentiating between "respectable" abortionists and those who were "butcher quacks." Those abortionists who were considered respectable were generally portrayed positively in the newspapers and other media of the time.[59]

Week Three: American History of Abortion

Questions

10. Reflect on the changes in the early 1900s. How are we seeing history repeat itself?

11. Why is it so hard to fight against abortion? What sins make abortion so attractive?

The 1950s–Today

Beginning in the 1950s, the general public began to consider that the problem wasn't abortion, but rather that abortion was illegal.[60] Some people began to imply that legal abortion would be better for society. This was the fruit of many decades of careful work on the part of the pro-abortion movement.

As society began to consider the idea of safely regulated abortion, Christians continued to speak out. In 1959, a Lutheran pastor, who, although he recommended contraception, strongly condemned abortion, said:

> The sin of willful abortion is widespread in the world today and among the American people, as we have seen; but when a sin has become common, its real sinful character may be overlooked. People no longer abhor an evil act if many people are guilty of it, and especially if it is found also among the so-called respectable classes. Christian women are surrounded by this spirit. They come in touch with women who have resorted to it. In times of distress or desperation or when a pregnancy has resulted from an unlawful relation, there is then the strong temptation to cover the former sin by another...The subject is delicate, but serious. Christian women must be instructed about its character and must be warned lest they, too, become guilty of it and burden their conscience with this sinful practice.[61]

Question

12. Unpack this quote a bit. What is this pastor saying? How does he recommend solving the problem of abortion among Christian women? Do our churches discuss abortion enough?

_____

_____

_____

_____

Roe v. Wade

In 1973, the Supreme Court decided in a 7–2 vote that the constitutional right to privacy (under the due process clause of the Fourteenth Amendment) extended to a woman's right to have an abortion.[62] Since this decision, abortion has been legal in all fifty states with some states restricting it to the first two trimesters (and lately some trying to restrict it to the first trimester) while others allow abortion up until birth. There are even states and politicians that are against protecting children born alive after an abortion attempt has been made.[63] This, as discussed earlier in this study, is infanticide.

Justice Harry Blackmun, the author of the Supreme Court's opinion on Roe v. Wade

Conclusion

The fight isn't over. The *Roe v. Wade* decision can be reversed. Each of us is responsible for not just making abortion illegal but making it unthinkable.

If you remember nothing else about this week, remember these things:

- Whenever you see abortion, you see the church stepping in to help people (more on this in a few weeks). This is our role as believers.
- The root cause of abortion is sin. If we can address the sin (whether it's adultery, fornication, or prostitution), we can prevent abortions.
- This is not an impossible fight, but it is a difficult one. The battle has been going on for centuries, and it can feel overwhelming. Don't give up! Soon we will start to explore how we can advance the cause of life.

Week Three: American History of Abortion

Things to Think About

- What shocked you the most about this week's lesson? What did you already know?
- What sort of cycle do you see in history? What would be the natural next step for us?
- What is our role in this? How can we bring about change in our country?
- Look at 2 Kings 21:1–2, & 6. Were nineteenth century pastors right in comparing abortion to the worship of Molech? How does this apply to us today?

Supplemental Information

If you have the opportunity, do some research on the Spiritist movement of the 1850s. Many of the ideals they embraced trouble our nation today. It can be helpful to realize that the problems we struggle with are not necessarily new. We must realize that societal corruption can be overcome. We are not destined to continue on the path we're on now.

Also interesting is that beginning in the 1860s, the *Times* did a number of pieces on abortion, showing that for the right price a woman could procure one. These abortions were condemned by the writers, and the exposure was meant to make the public aware of the horrors that were taking place.[64] This focus on public exposure could indicate that people were largely ignoring the practice and turning a blind eye to a great social ill. Books were written condemning abortion and calling for social justice, including *The Great Crime of the Nineteenth Century* (1867), *The Sexual Organism and Its Healthful Management* (1862), *The Science of the Sexes* (1870), and *The Physical Life of Women* (1870). In 1871, the *Times* complained that abortion was not prosecuted often enough, and shortly after that announcement shared a story of a woman who was killed during an abortion, stuffed into a trunk, and abandoned.[65] This media exposure came at the same time Christians were actively working to help women who were at risk for abortion. Never underestimate the power of media—or the power of willful ignorance. There are many people who, when faced with the reality of abortion, will decide to get involved.

NOTES

WEEK FOUR

Abortion in My State

Introduction

Each state has different laws concerning abortion. There are laws regarding minors, restrictions based upon gestational age of the baby, and sometimes there are exceptions for pregnancies resulting from rape and incest. Some states' laws are being challenged, and there are new bills being passed that further limit abortion or increase access to abortion.

Some states (including my home state of Pennsylvania) have horror stories and literal skeletons in their closets. Some of them are shifting to become more conservative while others are becoming more liberal. Some are working to regulate abortion clinics while others are working to regulate pregnancy medical centers.

You will have to look up information yourself to make sure you're getting the facts. This lesson will contain information regarding national laws as well as questions to help guide your research about your state. There is also a chart in the appendix with a summary of laws by state. Please realize that the laws are constantly changing. Double check to be sure this chart is still accurate for your state.

If you're outside of the United States, you'll need to find solid organizations that can provide good information. The questions posed here can help guide you, but you could be looking at a very different situation than what we're dealing with in the United States.

- National Right to Life (nrlc.org). This national organization has information on each state and also has affiliates in many states.
- The Guttmacher Institute (https://www.guttmacher.org/state-policy/explore/overview-abortion-laws). This is supposedly neutral but, in actuality, is pro-abortion.
- The Charlotte Lozier Institute (https://lozierinstitute.org/). This is a pro-life institute.
- Not sure where to look? Call your local pregnancy medical center. They will be able to point you in the right direction.

Related Scripture

What do we do when the laws of our nation are morally wrong? What are our options? As you review the laws of your state, you will realize that our country has laws that allow some people to kill other people. It's that simple. How do we respond to this? What is the right way to handle it?

Acts 5:29–32

But Peter and the apostles answered, "We must obey God rather than men. The God of our fathers raised Jesus, whom you killed by hanging him on a tree. God exalted him at his right hand as Leader and Savior, to give repentance to Israel and forgiveness of sins. And we are witnesses to these things, and so is the Holy Spirit, whom God has given to those who obey him."

Question

1. What is causing the apostles to recommend disobedience? How does this relate to abortion (Acts 5:17–26)?

___

Romans 13:1–7

Let every person be subject to the governing authorities. For there is no authority except from God, and those that exist have been instituted by God. Therefore, whoever resists the authorities resists what God has appointed, and those who resist will incur judgment. For rulers are not a terror to good conduct, but to bad. Would you have no fear of the one who is in authority? Then do what is good, and you will receive his approval, for he is God's

Week Four: Abortion in My State

servant for your good. But if you do wrong, be afraid, for he does not bear the sword in vain. For he is the servant of God, an avenger who carries out God's wrath on the wrongdoer. Therefore one must be in subjection, not only to avoid God's wrath but also for the sake of conscience. For because of this you also pay taxes, for the authorities are ministers of God, attending to this very thing. Pay to all what is owed to them: taxes to whom taxes are owed, revenue to whom revenue is owed, respect to whom respect is owed, honor to whom honor is owed.

Questions

2. What does Romans 13:1–7 mean in relation to abortion? What activities are acceptable and which ones would be wrong?

3. Is it ever permissible to act violently against an abortionist or a woman seeking an abortion? Should we use any means possible to end abortion, or are we limited by the law?

4. What do we do when our tax dollars go to pay for abortion services? Are we permitted to stop paying taxes?

1 Peter 2:13–17

Be subject for the Lord's sake to every human institution, whether it be to the emperor as supreme, or to governors as sent by him to punish those who do evil and to praise those who do good. For this is the will of God, that by doing good you should put to silence the ignorance of foolish people. Live as people who are free, not using your freedom as a cover-up for evil, but living as servants of God. Honor everyone. Love the brotherhood. Fear God. Honor the emperor.

Question

5. What was the emperor like at this time? Why would this have been difficult for early Christians to understand? How is our country sometimes like this today?

_____
_____
_____
_____

NATIONAL LAW & HISTORY OF ROE V. WADE

On January 22, 1973, the U.S. Supreme Court ruled that the general right to privacy includes a woman's right to have an abortion. The Court claimed that this right, while not explicitly stated in the Constitution, is inferred through other Constitutional provisions. When this decision was made, all state laws against abortion were voided.[66]

Roe's companion case, *Doe v. Bolton*, established that:

- States could not restrict a woman's right to obtain an abortion prior to viability of the unborn child.
- Abortion could be performed throughout all nine months of pregnancy. Ostensibly, abortions could only be performed to protect the health of the mother. However, instead of defining "health" as the absence of illness, the Court used a definition of health that encompassed not only physical health but also emotional health, familial health, and the woman's age. This broad definition allows for abortion on demand at any stage of pregnancy.[67]

Justices White and Rehnquist were the two minority votes. Justice Rehnquist wrote:

> To reach its result, the Court necessarily has had to find within the scope of the Fourteenth Amendment a right that was apparently completely unknown to the drafters of the Amendment. As early as 1821, the first state law dealing directly with abortion was enacted by the Connecticut Legislature. By the time of the adoption of the Fourteenth Amendment in 1868, there were at least 36 laws enacted by state or territorial legislatures limiting abortion. While many States have amended or updated their laws, 21 of the laws on the books in 1868 remain in effect today.[68]

Justice Rehnquist's statement tells us that the majority of lawmakers in our nation were not ready to legalize abortion on demand. Despite the state laws at that time, the Supreme Court felt it was appropriate to make a decision that affected billions of lives in devastating ways. Why take this all the way to the Supreme Court? Throughout the nation, passionate single-issue voters were determined to keep abortion illegal, and by 1973 it was clear to abortion advocates that changing the laws to increase access to abortion state by state would be slow, if not impossible.[69] Christians were doing their best to stop the advance of abortion. Believers knew that unfettered access to abortion would cause irreparable harm to our nation, and they were doing tremendous work to keep that from happening. In fact, prior to *Roe v. Wade*, they came extremely close to repealing the permissive abortion laws in New York.[70]

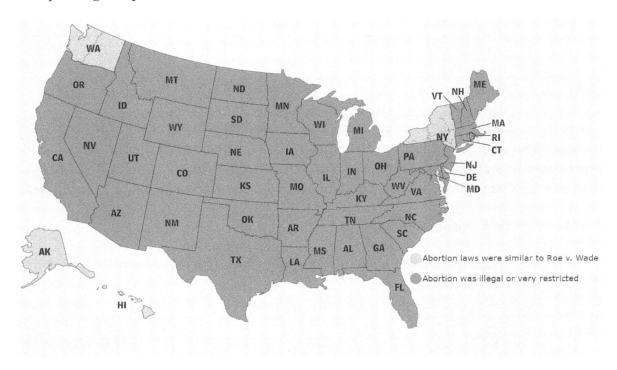

Above is a map of the United States. The four light colored states allowed abortion in some circumstances prior to the *Roe v. Wade* decision. The gray states had laws where abortion was completely illegal or restricted to cases such as physical risk to the mother or rape. *Roe v. Wade* adversely affected every state, especially the gray states. Instead of the states being allowed to determine their own approach to abortion, they were forced to comply with the decision of the Supreme Court.

What do abortion laws look like today? Go to the appendix and check out the charts from The Guttmacher Institute (guttmacher.org).

Questions

6. What were your state's laws prior to 1973? How did *Roe v. Wade* affect your community?

   _____
   _____
   _____
   _____

7. How did the abortion issue end up in the Supreme Court? Why did the pro-abortion movement choose to take this matter to a group of unelected individuals at the federal level instead of changing laws state by state?

   _____
   _____
   _____
   _____

8. Review the chart of different states' abortion laws in the appendix. What surprises you the most about different states' abortion laws? Did you know how variable they are? Which state is the most restrictive? Which is the least?

   _____
   _____
   _____
   _____

In Your State

Find out what laws govern abortion in your state. These are some questions to guide you as you do your research:

- How far along in pregnancy can a mother obtain an abortion?
- What exceptions could allow for an abortion later in pregnancy than the legal limit?
- Who, if anyone, must be notified before an abortion is performed?
- What protections are in place for minors seeking an abortion?
- What laws or regulations govern abortion clinics? How often are clinics inspected to ensure that they're complying?
- How many abortion clinics are in your state? Which is closest to your church? To your home?
- Are abortionists required to provide information about local resources, fetal development, and/or potential side effects to a mother seeking an abortion? Is

Week Four: Abortion in My State

there a waiting period? Are they required to provide follow-up care or have hospital privileges?

Questions

9. Is forcing abortion clinics to provide information about fetal development and the dangers of abortion to mothers seeking abortion helpful or not? Is there a way to ensure the mother receives the information in a sincere fashion?

   _____
   _____
   _____
   _____

10. Research the Kermit Gosnell case (WARNING: graphic content). What happened? Why did this cause new laws to go into effect? How can we prevent situations like this in the future?

    _____
    _____
    _____
    _____

Current Information

Like any current affairs topic, the landscape is constantly shifting. Rather than give potentially outdated information, here are some things you can check on:

- Have there been any recent changes in national law?
- Are there any pending laws in my state? What is their status? What is likely to happen in the future?
- How can my classmates and I affect our laws?

Conclusion

The purpose of this lesson is not to exhaustively review every stipulation in abortion law but to acquaint everyone with the laws in their state and their responsibility regarding those laws.

As Christians, we're required to be law-abiding citizens. This is difficult to do when a law violates our conscience. While there are no laws requiring us to obtain or participate in abortions, we must go beyond simply refusing abortion for ourselves and do everything we can to encourage mothers to choose life. It is our Christian duty to work to change the laws in order to protect the sanctity of human life.

Even though we may personally oppose abortion and work against it, we still carry responsibility for the sins of our nation. The concept of national guilt is not popular in our individualistic society, but it is one that we can't afford to ignore. When God punishes a nation, He does not necessarily single out the wrongdoers, and often those who are doing the right thing (or are unable to choose what they will do) will suffer along with those who committed the sin. Since we belong to a nation that allows abortions to take place, we bear responsibility for the suffering that those legal abortions have caused. The burden of this responsibility should galvanize us to change our laws.

Things to Think About

- Who was emperor at the time of Christ and shortly after? Do some research and find out who was ruling and what they were like. Does this have an impact on your understanding of 1 Peter 2:13–17?
- What would an "ideal" abortion law look like? What would it allow and what would it prohibit?
- If you could make one change in your state's abortion law, what would it be?

SUPPLEMENTAL INFORMATION

Morning-After Pill vs. the Abortion Pill

Have you heard of the abortion pill or morning-after pill? While these terms are tossed around with surprising frequency, there is some confusion about what they are and how they work. The term "abortion pill" typically refers to the drug RU486 that ends a child's life between five and seven weeks of pregnancy, or up to forty-nine days since the first day of the mother's last period. Some clinics now use it up to nine weeks of pregnancy, or sixty-three days since the first day of the mother's last period. This drug comes in two pills. The first pill is typically taken at an abortion clinic and the second is taken later, sometimes at home. The first pill, mifepristone, blocks the hormone the mother's body needs to provide nutrients for the baby. The second pill, prostaglandin, is taken two days later and induces labor.[71] There is a now a process where the mother can seek medical care and reverse the effects of the first pill. The abortion pill reversal process has already resulted in successful pregnancies and healthy babies.[72]

While RU486 is typically given at an abortion clinic, and presumably only after an exam has been performed and pregnancy has been confirmed, there has been a rise in what is being called "self-managed abortions" or, "at-home abortions." Women are now able to order these pills over the internet and take them at home. This is incredibly dangerous for both the mother and the baby. For more information, go to athomeabortionfacts.com.

The morning-after pill is quite different. There are several different morning-after pills, more accurately referred to as emergency contraceptives. Perhaps the most well-known emergency contraceptive is Plan B One Step®. This is a pill that must be taken within twenty-four hours of intercourse and is designed to prevent pregnancy. Because it could possibly do this by preventing a fertilized egg from implanting on the wall of the uterus, it is an abortifacient. Plan B and other medications are available in many places over the counter with no restrictions.

Viability

Research viability. When can an unborn baby survive outside the womb with medical intervention? When can they survive without medical intervention? How should this knowledge and changing technology impact abortion laws?

NOTES

WEEK FIVE

Eugenics

INTRODUCTION

Welcome to week five! This week we will cover eugenics and how it impacts us today. As with the history lessons, there is more to be said on this topic than what is in this guide.

Eugenics is an interesting and important subject. At its simplest, eugenics is the belief that the human population must be managed so it continues to evolve and become the best it can be. It is also the belief that the "better" people are more likely to limit their children than the "rank and file," thereby requiring those of higher intelligence to assist those of lower intelligence.

As discussed in week one, the precursor to hurting or killing someone is often the destruction of their humanity. God has put something inside us that abhors the idea of destroying human life, and in order to work past that we must convince ourselves that those we wish to destroy aren't human at all. Eugenicists used pseudoscience to promote the idea that some humans are more valuable than others. This pseudoscience provided the rationale needed to abuse and kill other human beings.

Why is this something to discuss in a study about our pro-life beliefs? We have been focused mostly on abortion up to this point, but it is essential for us to step back and look at why abortion presents the way it does. Why are abortion clinics primarily found in low-income areas? Why are low-income mothers more likely to abort than mothers with higher incomes? Why are people of color more likely to choose abortion?

While there are many factors that enter into each of these, some of the answers to these questions can be found by going back to the eugenics movement of the early 1900s. Many well-educated individuals were advocating some frightening ideas that were widely accepted in intellectual circles. You might say, "Come on, that was one hundred years ago! It's not happening today, not in our country." Well, people may not be as blunt about it as they were in the 1920s, but it is still happening, and we must be aware of it.

Question

1. How do you dehumanize others? Is it another race? Another age group? Someone from a different area or another religion? Ask God what you should do about this (John 13:16; Colossians 3:9–11).

   _____
   _____
   _____
   _____

DEFINITIONS

All definitions are taken from Webster's online dictionary.

Eugenics - a science that deals with the improvement (as by control of human mating) of hereditary qualities of a race or breed

Sterilization - to cause (land) to become unfruitful, to deprive of the power of reproducing…to make incapable of germination

RELATED SCRIPTURE

Genesis 1:28

And God blessed them. And God said to them, "Be fruitful and multiply and fill the earth and subdue it, and have dominion over the fish of the sea and over the birds of the heavens and over every living thing that moves on the earth.

God commands us to be fruitful and multiply. Eugenics, ethnic cleansing, and even the birth control movement find some of their roots in overpopulation theories. While we must care for the earth God has given us, He has also commanded us to fill it!

Week Five: Eugenics

Question

2. Look up the Malthusian Theory of Overpopulation. How does this theory impact us today? Did you or your children learn about this in school? How does this influence how we look at the poor and needy?

John 9:1–3

As he passed by, he saw a man blind from birth. And his disciples asked him, "Rabbi, who sinned, this man or his parents, that he was born blind?" Jesus answered, "It was not that this man sinned, or his parents, but that the works of God might be displayed in him."

Question

3. What does John 9:1–3 tell us about people with disabilities? How can our treatment of the disabled show "the works of God?"

Psalm 82:3

Give justice to the weak and the fatherless; maintain the right of the afflicted and the destitute.

Question

4. How does Psalm 82:3 conflict with the idea of eliminating the weak? How can we fulfill the responsibility of caring for those who are weak or destitute?

What Is Eugenics?

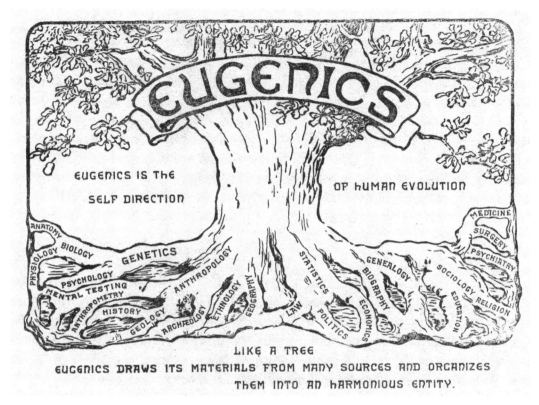

The logo from the Second International Eugenics Congress, 1921.

According to Ellsworth Huntington, the president of The American Eugenics Society in 1935, everyone in the American Eugenics Society agreed that "everything possible should be done to encourage large families in the right kinds of homes and to discourage them in undesirable homes."[73] Eugenics, therefore, is the science of improving the human population by encouraging some to reproduce and discouraging others. In its darkest forms, this included sterilizing, aborting, institutionalizing, or euthanizing (more on that later) those considered undesirable.

Who was considered undesirable? The quote below reviews the list of people targeted by two prominent eugenicists, Charles Davenport and Harry Laughlin:

> As a first order of business, Davenport and Laughlin published their top ten list of "degenerate protoplasm": (1) the feebleminded; (2) the poor; (3) alcoholics; (4) criminals; (5) epileptics; (6) the insane; (7) the "constitutionally weak"; (8) those suffering from venereal diseases; (9) the deformed; and (10) the deaf, blind, or mute…These 11 million people – according to the Eugenics Record Office – represented the bottom tenth of the U.S. population. The time had come to prevent them from reproducing.[74]

History of Eugenics

Because of time constraints, we will focus on eugenics in the 1930s and 1940s. This was the peak of the eugenics movement in the United Sates. Please note: eugenics, in one form or another, was around long before the 1930s. Throughout history, we see one people group working to exterminate another based on the idea that one group is superior to another.

Eugenics has existed throughout history in various forms, but in modern times it finds its roots in evolution.[75] The belief that humans are continuously evolving gives rise to the idea that we can encourage positive evolution by allowing the best and brightest to reproduce, while simultaneously preventing those deemed less worthy from reproducing. Charles Darwin made evolution famous with his book *On the Origin of Species* in 1859, and the phrase "survival of the fittest" appears a few years later in 1864 in Herbert Spencer's *The Principles of Biology*.[76] Spencer wrote that compassion was fatal to the human race. He said, "If they are not sufficiently complete to live, they die, and it is best that they should die."[77] What does that mean? Spencer is saying that it is acceptable for certain humans to be allowed to die, and that everyone else will be better off if they do. Darwin also applied evolutionary thought to the human race, but not before his half-cousin, Francis Galton. Galton coined the word "eugenics" in 1883 in his book *Inquiries into Human Faculty and Its Development*.

These works, and others, brought the pseudoscience of eugenics to the common American in the 1880s. The theory of the day was that modern civilization was allowing weaker humans to continue to reproduce instead of letting natural selection take place; bluntly, the weak were being prevented from dying of disease, injury, or starvation. To counter this process, early eugenicists believed society needed to step in and help evolution by preventing the weak from procreating. They believed that the ability of the weak or indigent to survive and reproduce was unnatural, and that it was society's responsibility to encourage natural selection. The eugenics movement picked up steam in the early 1900s and soon began to be studied all over the world.

Eugenicists used forced sterilization, contraception, and immigration limitation to prevent individuals from "inferior" races (such as the Irish) from entering the country and raising families. This material will focus on eugenics and sterilization, however, I encourage you to research eugenics and immigration/contraception on your own.

In the early 1900s, many state-level sterilization laws were overturned by higher courts, proving that there were people actively working against the eugenics movement. Even with these achievements, over sixty-four thousand individuals were forcibly sterilized in the United States between 1907 and 1963.[78]

Eugenics theory was widely accepted by American intellectuals in the 1930s and 1940s. Eugenics is still discussed today, though perhaps not as openly. Both the roots and the fruit of eugenics run contrary to the teaching of Scripture and wound the heart of God. As Christians, we must work hard to ensure that all life is valued, respected, and seen as equal.

Questions

5. How does eugenics counter the tenets of Christianity? Does it seem strange that the intellectuals of our nation could embrace such damaging philosophy?

_____
_____
_____
_____

6. Were you surprised to discover that so many individuals were forcibly sterilized in the United States? Why is it tempting to think that targeted sterilization might solve societal ills? How could these practices be abused?

_____
_____
_____
_____

Eugenics in Action

In his book *Tomorrow's Children*, Ellsworth Huntington hypothesizes that those in desirable homes should have large families while those in undesirable ones should have small or nonexistent families. He briefly considers the idea of the state bringing up children from parents he considered to be weak, but ultimately believed that heredity would prove too powerful. Additionally, women he considered to be superior (his term was "high grade") would be kept busy raising undesirable children, thereby lessening the likelihood that they themselves would reproduce and pass on their own genetics, genetics he considered to be superior.[79] Just like breeding dogs or plants, eugenicists believed it was possible to produce a superior quality of human by selecting for traits such as physical vigor, intelligence, and emotional stability.[80] It was also believed that physical superiority naturally went hand in hand with mental and moral superiority.[81]

WEEK FIVE: EUGENICS

Carrie Buck with her mother, Emma Buck.

How did eugenicists discourage undesirable people from reproducing? One method was forced sterilization.

Carrie Buck (photo at left) was considered feeble-minded, along with her mother and her child. The state of Virginia determined that she should no longer be permitted to reproduce. This case went all the way to the Supreme Court. Why? Those in power wanted a test case to prove that sterilization, with or without consent, was the law of the land.[82] It worked. The Supreme Court determined that Carrie should be forcibly sterilized. By 1934, twenty-eight of the forty-eight states had laws allowing forced sterilizations, and the Supreme Court ruling provided precedent for these sterilizations to continue.[83] And who determined who was to be sterilized? The government. While the patient or their guardians could object to the sterilization, this case (and others) show that it didn't mean the procedure wouldn't be performed. Forced sterilizations occurred in the US from the early 1900s until the 1970s. At the time of this writing, the *Buck v. Bell* ruling has not been reversed, meaning that if a state passed a law allowing forced sterilization, it would likely be upheld.

Justice Holmes shared the majority opinion of the US Supreme Court in *Buck v. Bell* (1927):

> We have seen more than once that the public welfare may call upon the best citizens for their lives. It would be strange if it could not call upon those who already sap the strength of the State for these lesser sacrifices, often not felt to be such by those concerned, in order to prevent our being swamped with incompetence. It is better for all the world if, instead of waiting to execute degenerate offspring for crime or to let them starve for their imbecility, society can prevent those who are manifestly unfit from continuing their kind. The principle that sustains compulsory vaccination is broad enough to cover cutting the Fallopian tubes…three generations of imbeciles are enough.[84]

Questions

7. What would happen if the government had the right to seize children from parents considered to be weak or inferior? How would these children, perceived as lower quality than their peers, be treated?

_____
_____
_____
_____

8. Are there states that would consider such a law today? What people groups might be targeted?

_____
_____
_____
_____

9. Do some research on Carrie Buck. Was she "feebleminded?" Should she have been sterilized?

_____
_____
_____
_____

Famous Eugenicists

Can you identify these famous eugenicists using these quotes and their images?

Can you guess who this eugenicist is based on this photo and the quotes to the right? Check the Teacher Guide for the answer!

The new government program would facilitate the function of maternity among the very classes in which the absolute necessity is to discourage it…[this program] brings with it, as I think the reader must agree, a dead weight of human waste. Instead of decreasing and aiming to eliminate the stocks that are most detrimental t the future of the race and the world, it tends to render them to a menacing degree dominant. [85]

Well, I think the greatest sin in the world is bringing children into the world—that have disease from their parents, that have no chance in the world to be a human being practically. Delinquents, prisoners, all sorts of things just marked when they're born. That to me is the greatest sin—that people—can commit. [86]

Can you guess who this eugenicist is based on this photo and the quotes to the right? Check the Teacher Guide for the answer!

Blood mixture and the resultant drop in the racial level is the sole cause of the dying out of old cultures; for men do not perish as a result of lost wars, but by the loss of that force of resistance which is contained only in pure blood. All who are not of good race in this world are chaff…[87]

Week Five: Eugenics

Can you guess who this eugenicist is based on this photo and the quotes to the right? Check the Teacher Guide for the answer!

Some day we will realize that the prime duty of the good citizen of the right type is to leave his or her blood behind him in the world; and that we have no business to permit the perpetuation of citizens of the wrong type.[88]

Question

10. Did any of these famous eugenicists surprise you? How do you think these individuals could have had a significant impact on both their contemporaries and society today?

___

Eugenics Today

While it's true that eugenics went out of style decades ago, many of its tenets are still being applied today. Birth control was an important tool of the eugenics movement, and today we see permanent and semi-permanent birth control being given to many young women, especially those in low-income areas. As another example of eugenics in action, in 2012 in New York City, over 6,500 more African American babies were aborted than were born.[89] Along similar lines, 79 percent of all Planned Parenthood abortion clinics are located within walking distance of African American and Hispanic communities.[90] Why do they target these communities? Take a look at The Negro Project. The Negro Project was developed by the intellectual white community in the 1930s and 1940s to push birth control and abortion in African American communities.[91] African Americans weren't even included in the project until it was well-developed. Does it sound helpful? Maybe on the surface, but it's important to realize that birth control (including abortion) is how eugenicists at that time wanted to limit people they considered undesirable from reproducing.

Here is another quote from Margaret Sanger regarding The Negro Project:

> His [an African American minister] work in my opinion should be entirely with the Negro profession and the nurses, hospital, social workers, as well as the County's white doctors. His success will depend upon his personality and his training by us. The minister's work is also important and also he should be trained, perhaps by the Federation [Planned Parenthood] as to our ideals and the goal that we hope to reach. We do not want word to go out that we want to exterminate the Negro population and the minister is the man who can straighten out that idea if it ever occurs to any of their more rebellious members.[92]

We're still coping with this racism today. The disproportionate number of abortions performed on minority mothers is shocking. Not to mention, it is very likely that some white mothers having abortions are carrying a child fathered by a person of color. In my home state of Pennsylvania in 2017, 53 percent of abortions were performed on women who self-identified as African American or Hispanic. Statewide, only 11.9 percent of women are African American and only 7.3 percent are Hispanic. Abortion disproportionately affects women and families of color. Margaret Sanger's legacy, Planned Parenthood, runs nine of the twelve largest abortion clinics in Pennsylvania. Even today, her organization is targeting families to destroy because of the color of their skin.[93]

Questions

11. How do the thoughts and policies of the eugenics movement affect us today? What does this say about the importance of studying history?

12. Have you heard people say things like, "It's better for a child to be aborted than to be born into a poor home," or, "They're better off dead than on welfare?" What do you think? Can children born into difficult homes succeed? What if they don't? Are they still valuable (Matthew 22:39; Matthew 19:14)?

Week Five: Eugenics

Conclusion

Like it or not, eugenics still impacts our lives today. While we would like to consign it to the past as a disturbing and uncomfortable relic, we would be foolish to believe that eugenics thought is a forgotten part of history. Eugenics is included with this curriculum because it is central to the philosophies of abortion and euthanasia. Those who fund, support, and promote abortion and euthanasia do so with a second goal in mind: to rid humanity of the "human weeds" of the world in order to free up space and resources for the rest of us. Does every abortion activist or proponent of euthanasia feel this way? Certainly not. However, eugenic philosophies lurk beneath the surface. To truly understand the culture of death we face, we have to understand the philosophy of eugenics, where it came from, and how it affects us today.

Supplemental Scripture

Job 24:14

The murderer rises before it is light that he may kill the poor and needy, and in the night he is like a thief.

Ecclesiastes 1:9

What has been is what will be, and what has been done is what will be done, and there is nothing new under the sun.

Mark 12:30–31

"And you shall love the Lord your God with all your heart and with all your soul and with all your mind, and with all your strength. The second is this: 'You shall love your neighbor as yourself.' There is no other commandment greater than these."

Things to Think About

- Why does the murderer prey on the poor and needy? Who are the poor and needy in our society?
- How does eugenics conflict with the command to love our neighbor as ourselves? Can we love someone we see as less valuable than someone else?
- What surprised you about this lesson? What did you already know?
- How do you see eugenics thought in everyday life?
- How should we as Christians counter these ideas?

NOTES

WEEK SIX

Euthanasia

INTRODUCTION

A topic that is frequently overlooked is euthanasia. This week we will focus on euthanasia in our society today instead of diving deeply into its history. That's not to say the history of euthanasia isn't worth studying, but with the prevalence of this movement in modern society, we simply won't have time to cover it here.

Euthanasia is often billed as a way for people to escape pain and suffering through what is known as the self-deliverance of suicide (whether assisted or independent).[94] Suicide, in any form, is a way for humans to take control of their lives by ending them in a manner of their own choosing. Journalist and author Derek Humphry, an influential proponent of assisted suicide, admits that there is no way to reconcile suicide and acknowledging God as Master of your fate. He writes in his book *Final Exit*, "If you consider God the master of your fate, then read no further. Seek the best pain management available and arrange hospice care."[95] He goes on to state that seeking to end your life is a way to take complete control of your life—and, more specifically, of your death.

The most common type of euthanasia in the news today is physician-assisted suicide. This is when a doctor prescribes a lethal dose of medication to a patient with the knowledge that the patient intends to use them to end their own life. In many ways, this is a new challenge for our country. We as Christians must act now to keep this ideology from taking hold. Many will say, "It's not that big of a deal," or, "It doesn't happen that often." Once is too often, and ending someone's life prematurely, even with their permission, is a big deal!

Questions

1. How does Christianity prevent us from being masters of our own fate? How does suicide (assisted or otherwise) indicate that we have no desire to submit to God (Hebrews 9:27; Job 14:5)?

   _____
   _____
   _____
   _____

2. What do you think about assisted suicide? What if the person is suffering? What if they desire to end their life? What if they asked you for help doing so?

   _____
   _____
   _____
   _____

DEFINITIONS

All definitions taken from Webster's online dictionary unless otherwise noted.

Murder - the crime of unlawfully killing a person especially with malice aforethought

Euthanasia - the act of killing someone rather than allowing them to die a natural death[96]

Passive Euthanasia - when a person removes an external item that keeps someone alive and allows them to die [97]

Active Euthanasia - participation by another individual in the killing of a person[98]

Involuntary Euthanasia - the killing of a person without their requesting it[99]

Suicide - the act or an instance of taking one's own life voluntarily and intentionally

Assisted Suicide - suicide committed by someone with assistance from another person; especially physician-assisted suicide

Week Six: Euthanasia

Physician-Assisted Suicide - suicide by a patient facilitated by means (such as a drug prescription) or by information (such as an indication of a lethal dosage) provided by a physician aware of the patient's intent

Utilitarianism - a theory that the aim of action should be the largest possible balance of pleasure over pain or the greatest happiness of the greatest number

Related Scripture

Genesis 2:7

Then the Lord God formed the man of dust from the ground and breathed into his nostrils the breath of life, and the man became a living creature.

God gives life. All of it. Life is a sacred gift, one that should be treasured. That indefinable spark is more than a beating heart or neurons firing in the brain—life can only be given by God. We need to draw a line and say that life can only be taken by God. We should never take life just because we think it's convenient. God and God alone should make this decision.

Exodus 20:13

You shall not murder.

We could stop right here, couldn't we? Exodus 20:13 makes it clear that God does not condone murder. It is not a stretch to use this verse to state that God doesn't condone suicide either. After all, just being angry opens us to God's judgment (Matthew 5:21–22)! God created us in His image (Genesis 1:27) and He knit us together in our mothers' wombs (Psalm 139:13). We are not to destroy His creation.

Question

3. Does the command "You shall not murder" from Exodus 20:13 cover the question of the morality of euthanasia? Why or why not?

   _____
   _____
   _____
   _____

Deuteronomy 30:19

I call heaven and earth to witness against you today, that I have set before you life and death, blessing and curse. Therefore choose life, that you and your offspring may live.

Here, the Israelites are told that if they obey God they will live, but if they follow other gods their lives will be shortened. Our culture is choosing other gods: the gods of security, wealth, health, and commercialism.

Question

4. Many would look at Deuteronomy 30:19 and say that God is threatening to curse his people. Is He? Or is He warning them of the inevitable consequences of sinfulness?

1 Corinthians 3:9–17

For we are God's fellow workers. You are God's field, God's building. According to the grace of God given to me, like a skilled master builder I laid a foundation, and someone else is building upon it. Let each one take care how he builds upon it. For no one can lay a foundation other than that which is laid, which is Jesus Christ. Now if anyone builds on the foundation with gold, silver, precious stones, wood, hay, straw—each one's work will become manifest, for the Day will disclose it, because it will be revealed by fire, and the fire will test what sort of work each one has done. If the work that anyone has built on the foundation survives, he will receive a reward. If anyone's work is burned up, he will suffer loss, though he himself will be saved, but only as through fire. Do you not know that you are God's temple and that God's Spirit dwells in you? If anyone destroys God's temple, God will destroy him. For God's temple is holy, and you are that temple.

Simply put, we belong to God. We are God's temple, and the Holy Spirit dwells in us.

Question

5. Take a moment and reflect on 1 Corinthians 3:9–17. Why are we holy? How should we treat ourselves (our bodies), and how should we treat others? Do we always behave as though we're God's temple?

WEEK SIX: EUTHANASIA

WRONG NO MATTER WHAT

This lesson will discuss the many abuses prevalent when euthanasia is allowed. Even if euthanasia always happened exactly the way it is intended, it is still immoral. It is wrong to kill another human and it is wrong to kill yourself. Just as bad, it is wrong to ask for someone else's assistance to end your life, and it is wrong to encourage someone (or refrain from discouraging someone) to end their life or the life of someone else.

Please don't fall into the trap that euthanasia and physician-assisted suicide can be regulated and are good ideas if done "correctly." There is no correct way to kill another human being.

Question

6. Why does euthanasia or assisted suicide seem harmless or even beneficial at first glance?

_____
_____
_____
_____

WHAT REALLY HAPPENS?

Derek Humphry, photo taken in 2012. Humphry was the founder of the Hemlock Society (now called Compassion and Choices) and the author of "Final Exit."

In his book *Final Exit*, Derek Humphry (the founder of the Hemlock Society, now called Compassion and Choices) relays a story about his first wife, Jean, that marks his entrance into the world of active euthanasia. Humphry writes that his wife desired to die, and he wanted to help her make that choice. He needed help, and in order to get it, he chose to work with a doctor that was not one of his wife's doctors. He claims in his book that he did this to avoid legal consequences for the doctors; if they chose to help him, they would be breaking the law. Instead, Humphry chose a doctor he remembered from his years as a reporter.

I called 'Dr. Joe' and asked if we could meet. He invited me to his counseling rooms, for he had by now become an eminent physician with a lucrative practice. As prestigious and powerful as he was, he still had not lost the compassion and humanity I had noted in earlier years. I told him how seriously ill Jean was and of her desire to die soon. He questioned me closely about the state of the disease, its effects on her, and what treatments she had undergone.

As soon as he heard that some of her bones were breaking at the slightest sudden movement, he stopped the conversation. 'There's no quality of life left for her,' he said. He got up from his desk and strode to his medicine cabinet.

Dr. Joe did some mixing of pills, and handed a vial to me. He explained that the capsules should be emptied into a sweet drink to reduce the bitter taste…A few weeks later, when Jean knew the time had come, she asked me for the drugs…fifty minutes later she stopped breathing.[100]

Question

7. Take some time to dissect this quote. What is wrong with this account? What are the obvious or potential abuses? How did the doctor know death was Jean's wish? How does anyone know it was her decision? Even if this account is completely accurate, where did they go wrong?

_____
_____
_____
_____
_____
_____
_____
_____

After Jean's death, Humphry chose to remarry. His second wife also died after ingesting a lethal dose of pills. In her suicide note, addressed to an anti-euthanasia friend, she confessed that Humphry told her that Jean did not die from the pills. Her note claims that Humphry held Jean down and suffocated her.[101]

Question

8. Do the claims of Humphry's second wife make a difference? If her note reflects what really happened, does it change anything?

_____
_____
_____
_____

WHAT'S THE TRUE MOTIVATION?

So why the big push? Why do we want the terminally ill to commit suicide early in their disease? Derek Humphry and Mary Clement wrote in their book *Freedom to Die: Politics and the Right-to-Die Movement*:

> A rational argument can be made for allowing PAS [physician assisted suicide] in order to offset the amount society and family spend on the ill, as long as it is the voluntary wish of the mentally competent terminally ill and incurable adult. There will likely come a time when PAS becomes a commonplace occurrence for individuals who want to die and feel it is the right thing to do by their loved ones. There is no contradicting the fact that since the largest medical expenses are incurred in the final days and weeks of life, the hastened demise of people with only a short time left would free resources for others. Hundreds of billions of dollars could benefit those patients who not only can be cured, but who also want to live.[102]

Allowing, and even encouraging, assisted suicide and euthanasia makes the healthcare business much more profitable. Instead of keeping people alive or caring for the ill, insurance companies can kill them quickly and avoid paying for the cost of their care.

WHERE THE ARGUMENT FALLS APART

Assisted suicide advocates use the either/or method to argue for suicide and euthanasia. For example, they may say something like, "Either a patient dies peacefully now or in agony later." They see each person's situation as hopeless, nothing more than a painful spiral toward an inevitable death. They do not discuss depression or its treatment, pain control, hospice care, or home care. They assume that if a person expresses a wish to commit suicide today, they will feel the same way tomorrow. Just like the push to legalize abortion, advocates state that legalizing assisted suicide will help regulate it and keep it safe (as though killing someone could ever be considered safe!).

Beyond the basic immorality of euthanasia, we must realize that the rosy picture painted by proponents of euthanasia is far removed from the reality of the situation. Oregon was the first state to legalize physician-assisted suicide in 1994. So far, Oregon has not documented any cases where patients were prescribed lethal pills because they were in unbearable pain. In fact, depression seems to be the strongest indicator that a person will request physician-assisted suicide. Even knowing this, only about 3 percent of people asking for help committing suicide were offered psychological services.[103]

This is only the tip of the iceberg. Who oversees the patient taking the lethal pills? Nobody does. Who ensures the pills are only taken by the patient and not by someone else? Nobody. Who checks to make sure the person isn't being pushed into choosing suicide? The law is supposed to, but practically speaking, this is almost impossible to know for sure. Just like with abortion, physician-assisted suicide is a dark and ugly practice.

Question

9. Do you see any other problems with euthanasia? What else could make this a very slippery slope?

___
___
___
___

Involuntary Euthanasia—Killing the Weak

Beyond the question of assisted suicide (where the victim presumably has control), we encounter the question of involuntary euthanasia. The difference here is that the person is unable or unwilling to consent, but someone else has decided that their life is no longer worth living. Not here, you might say, not in the United States! However, what happened with Terri Schiavo? Terri Schiavo was a young woman believed to be in a persistent vegetative state following cardiac arrest in 1990. What does that mean? Nobody is entirely sure. Her level of interaction and awareness was, and continues to be, a hotly debated topic. We do know that she was breathing on her own but required a feeding tube to receive the nutrients her body required. Terri's husband wanted her feeding tube withdrawn, but her parents were fighting to keep it in. The courts decided in favor of her husband, and her feeding tube was removed.[104] She was unable to consent to the removal of the feeding tube, and she was killed slowly by being deprived of food and water. Read that again. Terri was dehydrated and starved until she died.[105] Unfortunately, she is not a solitary case, and this happens much more frequently than what gets reported to the public. Humphry writes in his book, assuring his readers, "Take it from me, many hundreds of cases of active and passive euthanasia go undetected, or unreported."[106]

What is our responsibility toward those who are weak and dependent? To be truly pro-life, humane care must not be refused to any human at any time, regardless of their desire. This care includes warmth, food, water, cleanliness, shelter, etc. These are basic, non-medical essentials we all need. A patient may not refuse humane care or have such care refused for them. They may refuse medical intervention if they choose, but they may not refuse basic care such as food, water, and a safe and warm place to be. Does that mean that the patient must take a drink every time it's offered? No, and

in many cases, as death approaches, the patient may not be interested in drinking. However, water and food should not be denied them.

In contrast to that standard, society has been redefining humane care to say that food and water (especially if received through a tube) should be considered a medical intervention, not basic care—such was the case with Terri Schiavo. Some say that refusing food and water, especially if the patient had an advance directive indicating this, is ethical. We must realize that the provision of food and water, even when delivered through a tube, is not medical care but humane care, and should never be denied.

In contrast to our Christian duty to care for others and our grief when we learn of a suicide, the pro-euthanasia crowd celebrates individuals who choose death on their own terms. In *Final Exit*, Humphry discusses many ways to kill oneself. These include, but are not exclusive to, freezing to death, starving/dehydrating to death, and suffocating to death.[107]

Question

10. Should anything else, other than food, water, cleanliness, and warmth, be considered basic humane care? When is it okay to stop medical intervention? Why is this such a hard decision to make?

_____
_____
_____
_____

Who Is at Risk?

Who is most at risk of being euthanized or encouraged to commit suicide? The most vulnerable people groups are those with disabilities and the elderly. Why? Because they are often considered to be burdens on society. In a society such as ours that puts a high value on youth and vigor, we often believe that anyone who suffers should not be allowed to continue living. We must come to the place where we see all life as valuable, regardless of whether or not the person is young and healthy. God has given all of us life, and He has given all of us a purpose. Your purpose and abilities may be very different from those of someone with a disability, but that doesn't make you more important or valuable.

One of the first victims of the Holocaust was Baby Knauer. He was born blind and missing his leg and part of his arm. His parents were ashamed that they brought a "useless eater" into the world and asked permission to have him "put to sleep."

Permission for this was granted by Hitler himself.[108] Does this sound familiar? We are told that our babies with disabilities should not be allowed to suffer, and that it would be merciful to put them to death early on (usually before they're born).

Euthanasia is murder. Plain and simple. Murder is wrong and is an abomination in the eyes of God. As Christians, we must work to protect the weak, the aged, and the dying, and let them die the way God intends them to.

Question

11. Who, like baby Knauer, would be considered a useless eater today? Why does our society want to be rid of these people?

How Do We Protect Ourselves and Our Families?

- Go to patientsrightscouncil.org and get information on a Protective Medical Decisions Document (PMDD). This document will give the agent of your choice authority to act on your behalf and take legal action, if necessary, to ensure you and your rights are protected.
- If you or a loved one is being placed in hospice care, carefully research the facility and inquire about their connections with organizations such as Compassion and Choices (formerly the Hemlock Society). Pay close attention if a loved one verbalizes a desire to die—others may also be listening to them, and they may encourage death instead of appropriate counseling.
- Check the medical files of you and your dependents for a document labeled "Physician Orders for Life-Sustaining Treatment" (POLST). These can be filled out unknowingly (with the help of medical staff) and may conflict with and supersede other advance directives.
- Ask questions and insist on answers. Most medical providers are not interested in ushering you out of this world, but question medical procedures or policies that seem dubious. If you have an elderly or cognitively disabled relative or friend, help them get the answers they need.

- Be on the lookout for pro-euthanasia legislation and trends in our society. Educate yourself so you can help prevent euthanasia from becoming as widespread as abortion.
- Find out what your state's laws are. You could have a key role to play in protecting your loved ones and stopping, or preventing, euthanasia in your community.

Conclusion

Euthanasia is a growing threat in our country, and nobody is quite sure how bad it will be or what shape it will take. It is vital for our churches and communities to be aware of the language used to promote it and work to protect one another. The elderly and disabled are often easily forgotten, even by well-meaning believers. By valuing them, we can not only show them that they are loved and important, but we can show the world that they matter. The first step to an active euthanasia program is dehumanizing those who are to be euthanized. By doing our best to value others and treating their lives as sacred, we can turn the tide. The church (as a whole) can change the future, and this is an excellent place to start.

Things to Think About

1. How would you feel if friends and family were encouraging you to "make your own choice?" How would you feel if you knew you were expected to commit suicide to save your family grief and expense?
2. How can we educate our friends and family about this difficult subject?

Supplemental Scripture

2 Samuel 1 (text not included)

An Amalekite comes to David and asserts that he killed Saul because Saul asked him to and because he (the Amalekite) did not believe that Saul could continue to live. What was David's response? He executed the Amalekite for killing Saul. He certainly did not commend the Amalekite for killing his enemy, or even for killing someone who requested it and was likely going to die anyway. Although the Amalekite was lying to gain favor with David, his account was not one of war but of so-called mercy killing.

1 Corinthians 15:26

The last enemy to be destroyed is death.

Death is the enemy, yet the culture we live in embraces it. This is exactly the opposite of what God wants for us. Death is not a solution; it won't make things better. Death is not something we should seek for ourselves or others. As God said in Deuteronomy 30:19, we need to choose life!

2 Corinthians 12:9

But he said to me, 'My grace is sufficient for you, for my power is made perfect in weakness.' Therefore I will boast all the more gladly of my weaknesses, so that the power of Christ may rest upon me.

God's grace is enough for us. We are not to seek death; rather, we are to trust in God's grace and mercy.

Supplemental Questions

1. In 2 Samuel 1, do you think David would have reacted as strongly if the Amalekite had claimed to kill Saul in battle? Why or why not?

   _____
   _____
   _____
   _____

2. How does 2 Corinthians 12:9 show us that suffering can be positive? How can our suffering bring glory to God?

   _____
   _____
   _____
   _____

NOTES

WEEK SEVEN

Pro-Life Apologetics, SLED

INTRODUCTION

For some of you, this is the week you have been waiting for! Many people want to learn to better articulate and share their pro-life views with their friends and neighbors. This lesson focuses mainly on abortion, but the general principles can be applied to euthanasia as well. This is the beginning of the second half of the curriculum, but don't forget all you learned in the first half. Refer to the history lessons when discussing how to approach these topics today.

The world can be broken into three groups of people:

- There are those who are dedicated pro-lifers. These people believe in the sanctity of human life, and they're not changing their minds. They may or may not be educated about it, but you don't have to worry about converting them because they're already devoted to the cause of life.
- The second group is the dedicated pro-choicers. They're 100 percent committed to abortion, also with varying levels of education. While it can be interesting to engage them, you may not get very far.
- The third group is the one you're interested in. These are the people that aren't sure what they think, they haven't thought about it much, or they're wavering back and forth. These are the people you want to spend your time educating and encouraging. You can help these individuals come down firmly on the side of life.

WEEK SEVEN: PRO-LIFE APOLOGETICS, SLED

Question

1. What's your biggest frustration when discussing or debating abortion? What do you wish you could do better?

___

CAN YOU BE A NON-CHRISTIAN AND BE PRO-LIFE? CAN A CHRISTIAN BE PRO-CHOICE?

Many non-Christians are pro-life.[109] In fact, it is important that we make room for and welcome secular individuals into the pro-life movement. The pro-life cause is one of unity. The horror of abortion is something that must be stopped without worrying about whether we agree on every—or any—point of theology.

There are also Christians that are pro-choice.[110] We know that the pro-choice position does not stand up to Biblical argument, however, there is nothing to be gained by accusing these people of being nonbelievers. When discussing this topic with a Christian, use Biblical references and show them from our commonality of belief that the unborn must be protected.

Question

2. Can you serve alongside non-Christian pro-life people? What about Christian pro-choice people? Which do you think would be more difficult?

___

DEFINITIONS

All definitions taken from Merriam Webster's online dictionary

Apologetics - a systematic argumentative discourse in defense (as of a doctrine). A branch of theology devoted to the defense of the divine origin and authority of Christianity

Related Scripture

Proverbs 24:11

Rescue those who are being taken away to death; hold back those who are stumbling to the slaughter.

Rescuing those being taken away to death and those stumbling to slaughter is our responsibility as Christians. Part of this responsibility is educating those around us. A dedicated, kind, reasonable pro-life person can make a pro-choice person think, make an ambivalent person reconsider, and encourage another pro-life person in their convictions. Staying silent doesn't help anyone.

Question

3. Have you ever thought of yourself as a teacher? What people do you have the opportunity to teach? How is teaching part of fulfilling our duty outlined in Proverbs 24:11?

   _____
   _____
   _____
   _____

1 Peter 3:13–17

Now who is there to harm you if you are zealous for what is good? But even if you should suffer for righteousness' sake, you will be blessed. Have no fear of them, nor be troubled, but in your hearts honor Christ the Lord as holy, always being prepared to make a defense to anyone who asks you for a reason for the hope that is in you; yet do it with gentleness and respect, having a good conscience, so that, when you are slandered, those who revile your good behavior in Christ may be put to shame. For it is better to suffer for doing good, if that should be God's will, than for doing evil.

A gentle conversation can have a tremendous impact. Never underestimate the value of love and kindness.

We must always be prepared to make a defense for our beliefs, but we are to do it with gentleness and respect. Being harsh or judgmental is not going to sway anyone. In fact, sounding dogmatic and callous could drive someone away from the position you're trying to present! If you're known as a person who pushes your views and refuses to listen to others, you will be less effective at winning people to the cause of life. However, if you're known for being gentle, loving, and kind, you are more likely to be successful at encouraging others to rethink their position.

Question

4. Is it hard to approach the subject of abortion the way we're instructed to in 1 Peter 3:15? Why or why not? Do you struggle with approaching difficult topics gently and in love?

___
___
___
___

2 Timothy 2:24–26

And the Lord's servant must not be quarrelsome but kind to everyone, able to teach, patiently enduring evil, correcting his opponents with gentleness. God may perhaps grant them repentance leading to a knowledge of the truth, and they may come to their senses and escape from the snare of the devil, after being captured by him to do his will.

Be kind to *everyone* and be able to teach. All of us are called to teach, whether to groups or individuals. You can be an instrument of change in someone's life, but in order to do that you have to educate yourself and commit yourself to gentleness.

Question

5. What does 2 Timothy 2:24 mean when it tells us to "not be quarrelsome but kind to everyone?" How should this impact every area of our lives? How does this make us more courageously pro-life?

___
___
___
___

The Pro-Choice Argument

The core of the pro-choice argument is not necessarily that an unborn child is not human, rather it is that the unborn child is somehow less human than the mother. Therefore, the mother's wishes and rights supersede those of the child. Closely connected with this is the idea that abortion is a private decision, one that nobody else has a right to make for another person. They would say it's fine to be pro-life, but you can only make those decisions for yourself, not for anyone else.

The pro-choice movement has invested a great deal of time and money into developing and promoting talking points. These are short, memorable phrases that are frequently repeated to the point that they are commonly accepted as fact. When you engage others in a discussion about abortion (even those who don't have a definite opinion on the subject), they will often spit out these talking points simply because they've heard them again and again.

Pro-Choice Talking Points

- My body, my choice.
- Abortion is a choice between a woman and her doctor.
- Women need to make the responsible choice that is right for them.
- The chances of death or injury in childbirth are higher than the chances of death or injury during an abortion.
- Outlawing abortion will just force women to go back to illegal and dangerous back-alley abortions. Abortion should be safe, legal, and rare.
- Outlawing abortion will cause women who suffer miscarriages to go to jail. Even worse, women will be forced to carry a rapist's child to term.

Pro-Life Counterpoints

- Human life is sacred from conception to natural death. An unborn child has its own DNA, its own blood type, and its own organs. While the child resides within the mother, he/she is not part of the mother's body.
- It is up to society to protect the weakest among us. The unborn can't speak for themselves, so we must speak for them. This is not a decision that should be made in private.
- Women suffer from an abortion emotionally, physically, and spiritually.[111] The legality of abortion often makes them feel as if they must consider the option, even when they don't want to. Even pro-choicers will admit that abortion is often a painful and difficult decision.[112]
- Abortion injuries and deaths are underreported.[113] Also, it's important to consider the fact that women are more likely to engage in destructive behavior after an abortion than they are after childbirth.[114]
- Abortion is legal, but it is neither safe nor rare. Not for the mother and certainly not for the child. Mothers need real help, not abortion.
- Even when abortion was illegal, the mother was rarely prosecuted (see week three). Instead, prosecution focused on the abortionist. So why would a mother

suffering a miscarriage be put in jail? While many people would say that rape and incest are reasons for abortion, we must remember that the child is still a person who deserves to live. Furthermore, abortion can be used to cover up crimes like rape, incest, and sex trafficking, and abortion can inflict more trauma on the already traumatized mother.[115]

Question

6. What are the pro-choice arguments you hear the most? Which is the hardest to refute? Why are talking points so hard to combat?

___
___
___
___
___

Pro-Life With Exceptions

When we discuss abortion, there will always be someone who will bring up exceptions. They'll say, "I'm against abortion—unless the mother was raped," or, "I'm against abortion except for situations where the mother's health or life is at risk." Why do we allow these exceptions? Because if we say we are against abortion in these circumstances, it makes us sound callous and cruel. Even though we're pro-life, perhaps we believe there are some instances where the threat to the physical or psychological health of the mother overrules the child's right to life.

Remember, deciding to focus on the majority of abortion cases is not the same as conceding the humanity of a child conceived in rape. Pictured here is Rebecca Kiessling with her three daughters. Rebecca was conceived in rape, and her life matters!

The easiest thing to do with these exceptions is to choose to set them aside for the sake of discussion. The cases of rape, incest, and life of the mother are rare; only 3 percent of all abortions occur because of rape, incest, or to preserve the mother's life or health.[116] Often, to simplify the argument, it's easier to say, "Let's not worry about the 3 percent of abortions resulting from rape, incest, and danger to the mother right now. Let's focus on the other 97 percent." By discussing abortion in all other circumstances, it can help clear the air and allow the discussion to proceed. Does that mean these exceptions aren't worth discussing? Absolutely not. We will dive more deeply into these tough questions in week nine.

If you do want to discuss the exceptions, go for it. Remember to focus on the humanity of the child and extend compassion to the mother. We would never justify killing one person to benefit another, yet this is a common argument for abortion. Also, keep in mind that children conceived in rape and incest, or those that were a threat to their mother's lives, are real people. They matter. Don't dehumanize them.

This week, our focus is on defending the pro-life position in general. Later on, we will dig into some of these special cases.

Question

7. Do you believe there are circumstances that justify an abortion? Which ones?

_____
_____
_____
_____

Defending Life, SLED

Debunking pro-choice arguments can be exhausting and maddening. You show facts proving the unborn are separate humans from their mothers and the person argues that the unborn aren't sentient. You say women shouldn't have the option of abortion and they paint you as heartless and cruel. Stephen Schwarz, author of *The Moral Question of Abortion*, created a method for stating the pro-life position clearly and succinctly. It was popularized by Scott Klusendorf, the founder and president of Life Training Institute.

In this model, the best approach is to keep the focus on the unborn child and not follow any rabbit trails. Is the unborn human? If the answer is yes, are they as human as everyone else or somehow less human? You can then discuss the danger of considering some to be less human than others and where that can take us. (You can use examples such as slavery and the Holocaust.)

Philosophically, there is no difference between the adult you are today and the fetus you were years ago. You're the same person with the same rights. The best way to remember and articulate this position is with the acronym SLED:

S – Size

L – Level of Development

E – Environment

D – Degree of Dependency

S – Size

Size doesn't equal value. Are tall people more valuable than short people? Men are usually larger than women; does that make them more of a person? The unborn child is smaller than an adult and often smaller than a newborn, however, size is not a reason to say that someone is more or less valuable than someone else.

L – Level of Development

Is an embryo or fetus less developed than an adult? Yes. But children and teens are also less developed than full-grown adults. Are newborns less human than adults? Are teens? People go through various stages of development throughout their lives, but regardless of what stage they're in, they are not more or less human than someone else.

E – Environment

Were you human outside this building? When you came inside, did you remain human? Are you sure? Of course! Traveling down the birth canal is not a magical humanizing process. If it were, C-section babies would be in trouble! A baby is a baby, whether in the womb or out of it. Birth, while it is a momentous occasion, is not developmentally significant.

D – Degree of Dependency

One of the biggest pro-choice arguments is that women can have abortions because the child depends on them for life and they shouldn't "be forced to have a baby they don't want." What about people on insulin? Dialysis? Oxygen? Lots of people are dependent on different things and other people. That doesn't make them less human. Remember, pregnancy only lasts for nine months. Is the mother's discomfort for a short period of time more important than the child's life?[117]

Focus on the Mother

What do we, as courageously pro-life Christians, believe? We believe that **every mother has the right to love and support during an unexpected pregnancy.** This phrase can be used to answer many pro-choice arguments. Women need love and support, they don't need abortion. Dig down to the root of the problem: why are women choosing abortion? Is it fear? Lack of resources? Abuse? The problem is *not* the baby. Let's identify and solve the real problems.

Absolute Truth

Abortion is morally wrong. We, as Christians, believe in right and wrong. We also believe there is an objective standard to measure right and wrong—the Bible. Being pro-life isn't an opinion. An example of an opinion is someone liking candy better than cake. Candy isn't morally superior to cake, it's just different. It doesn't hurt anyone to have a preference. However, saying, "You think abortion is wrong and that's your opinion, but you can't force it on someone else" is erroneous. If abortion is wrong, it's wrong for everyone, not just some people. What about rape? Murder? Spousal abuse? Are they wrong for everyone or just wrong for some people? When an action causes harm to someone else, it's no longer a matter of opinion, and those being harmed are worthy of protection.

Things to Think About

- Does debating or discussing abortion make you uncomfortable? Why? Spend some time pondering this question. If you can find the root of your discomfort, you will have an easier time overcoming it.
- Why do discussions about abortion almost always jump to extreme cases such as rape? Why is it hard to stay on track when having a discussion?
- Are there other situations where the welfare or the life of one person is competing with the comfort or convenience of another? How do we as a society deal with this? Is it acceptable to expect one person to forego comfort and convenience to save the life of another?

Conclusion

Defending your beliefs on any topic may sound like torture to you. Some people thrive on conflict while others avoid it at all costs. Know that there is a way to defend your pro-life beliefs without arguing or becoming aggressive. In fact, the gentler the approach, the more likely it is to succeed. Focus on loving the person in front of you as much as you love an unborn child. Help others see the value of their own humanity and help them transfer that value to an unborn child, someone with disabilities, or an elderly person. Don't back down from the truth but present it in a way others can understand.

Are you someone that thrives on a good debate? Don't forget that the person you're debating has the same value as the unborn children you're so passionate about! The goal of a debate is not to "win"; it's to present the truth. Whatever your personality, you can do this! Remember, the Bible tells us in 1 Peter 3:15 to "honor Christ the Lord as holy, always being prepared to make a defense to anyone who asks you for a reason for the hope that is in you; yet do it with *gentleness and respect*" (emphasis added).

Ready for next week?

Go to http://prolifetraining.com for more info. Also, there are books listed in week ten that can help you prepare for next week. This lesson is the barest overview; there is much more to learn.

Next week we're going to put these arguments to the test, so get ready!

NOTES

Pro-Life Apologetics, Practice

INTRODUCTION

Welcome to week eight! This is the week you get to use the skills you've been learning. Don't just rely on this curriculum! Prepare yourself by doing some research on your own.

- Read articles from the pro-choice point of view. Engage family and friends who disagree with you. Don't try to argue with them, just listen and learn where they're coming from.
- Look up Scott Klusendorf or other pro-life apologists on YouTube. Many good debates have been recorded and posted there.
- Visit prolifetraining.com. They have a fantastic website dedicated to defending the pro-life position.
- Review the rules for the class. Someone in your class may be pro-choice; they do not need you attacking them. Practice being kind!

Things to Think About

- How can my words affect someone who has been involved in an abortion decision? If the person I am debating has had an abortion, will that change what I say? Why or why not?

- What's more important during a debate: being right, or encouraging the other person to rethink their views?
- Do I think that some people are "lost causes?" How can I combat this attitude of defeatism?

Conclusion

Defending our beliefs is a skill that most individuals lack. It can be intimidating and uncomfortable, so we generally avoid it. Do your best to continue practicing outside of class. If you're struggling, continue role-playing with someone from your church. You might feel silly, but it really makes a difference. As with anything else, the more you know and the more you practice, the more comfortable you'll feel. By developing the skill of apologetics you'll be able to not only defend your beliefs concerning life, you'll be able to clearly articulate your beliefs in other areas. Whether or not this is your gift, you can do this. Don't give up!

NOTES

WEEK NINE

Beyond the Debate: Discussing Tough Topics with Love

Introduction

Welcome to week nine! Our discussion this week is twofold. First, we'll discuss the tough questions. What about abortion when the mother has been raped? What about when her life or health are at risk? What if the baby has been diagnosed with a condition that will result in a difficult, painful, or shortened lifespan?

Second, we'll learn that having all the right arguments won't win people to the pro-life viewpoint if we forget that the person we're talking to matters. It's not just about facts, statistics, fetal development, and knowing the right Bible verses. Winning someone to the side of life will only happen when we truly listen to the people we're talking to and understand where they're coming from. Why are they pro-choice? Why aren't they sure about their stance on abortion? Don't just listen to answer, listen to understand.

> "I changed my mind about being pro-choice because someone lectured me about facts and paid no attention to me as a person."
>
> *- Said No One Ever*

Related Scripture

How did Jesus reach people? Who did He focus on? As we discussed in week one, Jesus reached out to people with the truth in love, and He often did so individually. Yes, he spoke to crowds, but there are many examples throughout the Gospels of Him taking time to reach people one-on-one. Many of these people would have been considered the "undesirables" of society, but He still took time to speak with them.

Question

1. How can we be like Jesus when we're talking to people about this sensitive topic? How is it difficult to approach this topic gently and with love (John 4:16–30; John 8:1–11; Luke 19:1–10)?

_____
_____
_____
_____

John 4:16–30

This woman could be a modern-day woman at the well. How do we feel about her? Is this someone we would want to walk up to and chat with?

Jesus said to her, "Go, call your husband, and come here." The woman answered him, "I have no husband." Jesus said to her, "You are right in saying, 'I have no husband'; for you have had five husbands, and the one you now have is not your husband. What you have said is true." The woman said to him, "Sir, I perceive that you are a prophet. Our fathers worshiped on this mountain, but you say that in Jerusalem is the place where people ought to worship." Jesus said to her, "Woman, believe me, the hour is coming when neither on this mountain nor in Jerusalem will you worship the Father. You worship what you do not know; we worship what we know, for salvation is from the Jews. But the hour is coming, and is now here, when the true worshipers will worship the Father in spirit and truth, for the Father is seeking such people to worship him. God is spirit, and those who worship him must worship in spirit and truth." The woman said to him, "I know that Messiah is coming (he who is called Christ). When he comes, he will tell us all things." Jesus said to her, "I who speak to you am he." Just then his disciples came back. They marveled that he was talking with a woman, but no one said, "What do you seek?" or, "Why are you talking with her?" So the woman left her water jar and went away into town and said to the people, "Come, see a man who told me all that I ever did. Can this be the Christ?" They went out of the town and were coming to him.

This is an incredibly powerful passage of Scripture. We tend to smooth over Bible characters and forget how raw and tough they were. This woman would not have been easy to talk to. She chose to go to the well by herself. Why? Probably because nobody wanted to talk to her. She was likely well-known in her small town. She had been with many men and was almost certainly despised by the other women of the town. Not only that, she was a Samaritan *and* a woman! Certainly nobody a self-respecting Jewish male would talk to.

What was her life like? Was she abused? Was she living with a disease? Was she being sold for sex? Whatever her story, I can't imagine she was easy to love. However, even with all her issues, the God of the universe chose to reveal Himself to her. He chose to speak with her alone. He could have gone to the leaders of the village. He could have gone to the well during the busy time and paid attention to the upright wives and their beautiful children. Instead, he chose this woman.

Abby Johnson is a good example of someone a pro-life person wouldn't have wanted to talk to. In her book *Unplanned,* she describes her involvement with Planned Parenthood and how she ended up running an abortion clinic. Because of consistent, loving, pro-life people and the power of the Holy Spirit, Abby became pro-life and now runs a ministry working to help people leave the abortion industry. In some ways, Abby is a modern-day woman at the well, someone many Christians would want nothing to do with, somebody who could be tough to love. However, God has used her in amazing ways, and all of it happened because people cared enough to reach out.

Questions

2. What would the woman at the well, described in John 4:16–30, look like today? Would she be someone we would want to talk to? Someone we would spend time with?

___
___
___
___

3. How did Christ change the world (or her part of the world) by talking with her? How did she become a voice for the gospel? How can people we talk to change more hearts than we could on our own?

___

___

___

___

The Tough Cases

Debating abortion is hard enough, but when you add a problem like rape, incest, or a life-threatening pregnancy, it becomes nearly impossible. How do we approach situations like these without sounding cruel or callous?

Rape and Incest

We can all agree that no woman should be raped or molested. However, what happens when a woman is sexually assaulted and becomes pregnant from that assault? First, realize that rape is incredibly traumatic. Abortion is also traumatic. Adding an abortion to a rape is not going to lessen a woman's pain or trauma. Second, the baby did absolutely nothing to earn the death penalty. Is allowing abortion in cases of rape a pro-life position? Ask Rebecca Kiessling,[118] Ryan Bomberger,[119] or Pam Stenzel.[120] Each of these people were conceived in rape, and they certainly aren't the only ones. Regardless of whether or not a baby grows up to become an amazing pro-life advocate like those mentioned, every individual deserves to live. A baby conceived in rape is no less human than one conceived in love. Not only that, but we must ask ourselves this: does abortion solve anything? No. Abortion is never a good solution. The victim of rape needs love, support, assurance, and, if she chooses, an adoptive family for her child. She does not need an abortion.

This is the reality: once a woman has been raped and finds she is pregnant, there is no good solution. Through no fault of her own, she is now faced with carrying a child to term and delivering. This experience will be painful, awkward, inconvenient, and potentially life-threatening. Even if she chooses to make an adoption plan for the baby, she will be physically and emotionally changed forever. We might think, what right do we have to insist that someone go through this? The pregnancy occurred against her will, why should she suffer?

Unfortunately, life is often unfair. Victims suffer because of the choices of their attackers, and survivors of rape and incest are no different. Once conception has occurred and a new life has been formed, it is necessary for the mother to carry that child to term and deliver. That may sound harsh, but a child's life is at stake. The mother needs all the love, help, and support we can give her, both before and after delivery, but abortion is not the answer.

Life/Health of the Mother

What about situations where the life or health of the mother is at stake? In some ways, this dilemma can be more difficult to deal with than rape or molestation. What do you do when the mother is going to die because she is carrying a baby? What about a circumstance that threatens the life of the baby as well? The Dublin Declaration, a statement signed by over 1,000 medical providers, says it well:

> As experienced practitioners and researchers in obstetrics and gynecology, we affirm that direct abortion – the purposeful destruction of the unborn child – is not medically necessary to save the life of a woman. We hold that there is a fundamental difference between abortion, and necessary medical treatments that are carried out to save the life of the mother, even if such treatment results in the loss of life of her unborn child. We confirm that the prohibition of abortion does not affect, in any way, the availability of optimal care to pregnant women.[121]

A pregnant woman is often able to receive treatment for whatever is wrong with her. That treatment *may or may not* have side effects for the baby. The decision must be carefully made—how much risk is acceptable for the mom and how much is acceptable for the baby? But to say the baby must be killed to avoid birth defects resulting from treatment or medication simply doesn't make sense. The quote above is correct; some treatments (such as treating an ectopic pregnancy) can result in the loss of an unborn child. The key goal is to treat the mother, not kill the child.

Our intentions matter. If we approach a pregnant woman with the intention of treating her illness, that is very different from approaching her with the intention of killing her child. Pregnant women facing life-threatening complications must be treated. At no time should a woman be told that she can't have life-saving medication or treatment because she is pregnant. Could harm result? Yes, it could. The baby could end up with any number of issues or the mother could miscarry. Choosing to treat the mother doesn't mean we don't care about the child. It means we care about both, and the health of each needs to be carefully weighed.

Adverse Prenatal Diagnosis

What about a situation where the baby is diagnosed in utero with something that will kill him or her during or shortly after birth? Or, what if they're diagnosed with a disability that will cause them to be a burden or to live a difficult life? We must remember that ALL life is valuable and precious. We cannot destroy someone because they're inconvenient or difficult. People deserve to live the life God intended for them, even if it's shorter than we would like it to be. This is similar to the euthanasia debate—life is valuable even if it isn't what we think it should be. Killing a child in utero because they may die after birth is wrong.

A quick internet search will turn up plenty of firsthand accounts of parents who chose to abort their children rather than risk delivering a child with special needs. These stories are often heart wrenching, but it is important that we see what's really going on. There is often an aversion to having a child that is less than perfect. Sometimes it could be something as simple as a club foot or a cleft palate. Other times, it could be as devastating as anencephaly or trisomy 18. Regardless, we are not to set ourselves up as mini-gods that determine who should live and who should die. Until a child's heart stops beating, they must be protected. Could that be hard for the mother, to carry a child that will surely die at delivery? Yes, that is incredibly difficult. However, killing the child to prevent heartache is unacceptable. In situations like these, abortion is often presented as a way to save the child from pain and suffering. Is that our job? Should we kill people to spare them from pain? No. God is in charge of giving and taking life, not us.

Questions

4. What do you think about these exceptions? Could you answer someone regarding these topics?

   _____
   _____
   _____
   _____

5. What support can we offer a mother facing an adverse prenatal diagnosis? What about a family that is about to welcome a child with significant physical or developmental disabilities?

   _____
   _____
   _____
   _____

The Case for Courage

It's hard when a friend or family member tells you they're suffering. We want to solve the problem, to make it all go away. What do you do when it looks like abortion is the only option? Your daughter has everything going for her and the boy is a loser—would abortion be okay then? Your sister is in pain every day because of her pregnancy. Maybe she's on bed rest, depressed, or anxious. What about then? Your best friend was raped on a date. She didn't turn him in and now she's pregnant. Now what?

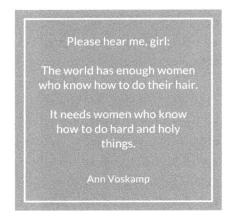

Take courage. Tell them that the right decision is not always the easy decision. Sometimes we're called to do hard things, painful things, difficult things. Our job is not to offer them an easy way out—it's to stand beside them during the hard times. The message they need is not, "I'll support you if you choose abortion." They need to hear you say, "Abortion is wrong. I love you too much to help you make that decision. I know you're facing a tough road, and I will be there for you every step of the way. You can do this."

Question

6. Have you ever had to deal with a difficult situation like rape, incest, or a pregnancy that endangers the mother? How could your stance on life change if it was you or someone you know suffering?

_____
_____
_____
_____

What If My Friend Wants an Abortion?

It's all well and good to talk about abortion in the abstract. You can learn about it and perhaps even debate it, but what do you do when abortion affects you personally? What if your friend, daughter, cousin, acquaintance, coworker, or even a stranger tells you they want to get an abortion?

You might panic. What do you do? What do you say? You know you don't want to help them get an abortion, but how do you stop them?

First, realize that in this country they have the right to obtain an abortion, even though we do not agree with this. You can talk to them and encourage them to choose life, but the choice is ultimately theirs. Your responsibility is to educate and encourage. You can't force them to do what you want them to do. (The exception to this would be children who are minors. If your daughter is a minor, she likely needs your signature to obtain an abortion—don't sign, and don't allow her father to sign either.)

Second, know that you won't have all the answers, and that's okay! Instead of trying to come up with an answer to every problem or question, simply be there. If you can help, help. If not, listen. Understand. Sympathize. Once they see that you love them, they will be more open to your suggestions.

Third, encourage them to make an appointment with their local pregnancy help center. If you are able to, go with them. Let them know you're there for them no matter what. Give them a ride if they need it, or maybe babysit their other children so they can focus on what the pregnancy center staff are saying.

Finally, commit to being there for them long-term. If they choose to continue their pregnancy, they might need help for years to come. You can be present with them all along the way.

No matter what, don't be involved in their abortion. If they decide to have an abortion, you should continue to love them, but that doesn't mean you drive them to the clinic, help pay for it, or support the procedure in any way.

Above all, pray for them and their child. God is still doing miracles! Even when all hope seems lost, pray.

Questions

7. Have you ever had a friend or relative talk to you about obtaining an abortion? What did you do? What do you wish you had done differently?

_____
_____
_____
_____

Week Nine: Beyond the Debate: Discussing Tough Topics with Love

Why Pro-Life/Pro-Choice?

Why would someone want to be pro-life?

Think about it. What would induce someone to change their viewpoint and agree with you? Here are some possible reasons:

- When they were in a tough spot, pro-life people helped them.
- They truly love women and their children and want to make a difference.
- They see that the majority of pro-life people are loving and caring.
- They understand that an unborn child is a human.
- They want to make a positive difference.

More importantly, why would someone want to choose life for their baby? A great deal of what we say has nothing to do with the words that come out of our mouths. Yes, words are important. We must know what we're talking about. However, people will be more interested in hearing what we have to say if they see something positive in how we act. Are pro-life people hateful or are they loving? Do they strive to protect others or are they spewing angry rhetoric? The pro-life cause is one that will be won with love, not with arguments.

Why would anyone want to be pro-choice?

It's important to understand why someone chooses a certain position. Once you know why, you can be more effective in countering their arguments.

We've reviewed the arguments and reasons for being pro-life, but why would someone choose to be pro-choice? Here are some common reasons why people choose to be pro-choice:

- They may be reluctant to impose morality on another person. Our society focuses on the individual. Whatever you want to do, or whatever feels right, you should do—and nobody has the right to stop you. However, the Bible tells us there is right and wrong. What's wrong for one person (i.e. sin) is wrong for everyone. This type of person may be pro-life for themselves but might not think they have the right to insist that anyone else choose life. If someone you know genuinely believes abortion is wrong but they're reluctant to take a stand, help them see that the unborn are worthy of legal protection. Show them that abortion hurts women. Encourage them to be part of making a difference.
- They may sincerely believe the rhetoric and talking points of the pro-choice movement. It may be all they've ever heard. Perhaps they've never seriously

thought about the pro-choice position. As you ask questions about their views, they may realize that they don't fully understand what they believe. Gently allow them to come to the conclusion on their own. Your goal is to get them thinking.
- They may truly believe that abortion is something women need and should be able to get whenever they want. This is the hardest person to talk with. They may become angry and hurl accusations at you. Always respond with love. You don't know why they are so adamant, it could be…
- They may have an abortion in their past. Often the most passionate defenders of abortion are deeply hurt because they had an abortion or participated in an abortion in their past. This person may never admit to the abortion, or if they do they may never say that they struggle with it. They may even insist that it's no big deal. Whether or not they seem to be bothered by it, make sure you behave as though they are hurting. Do not tell them how to feel, but be gentle with your words. Don't rush in with, "It's okay," or, "You didn't know better." Lovingly acknowledge the sin and quickly follow up with the message of hope and forgiveness. Regardless of who you're talking to, assume that someone within earshot has been through an abortion or participated in an abortion. Always approach the topic with love and the message of forgiveness.

Each of these people should be approached individually, gently, and with love. The pro-choice movement is full of angry, bitter people who are certain we're trying to take away their rights and destroy their lives. What if we made the pro-life movement attractive by our words and actions? What if we were known as loving, gentle, truthful people?

Question

8. Does this lesson change how you approach pro-choice people or people who are unsure about their beliefs? If so, how?

_____
_____
_____
_____

The Bottom Line

Being pro-life is about loving people. All people. If we're talking about a difficult circumstance, we need to do it with love. If we're talking about a past abortion, we need to do it with love. We must love both those who have been born and those who are unborn. Even if they don't love us, believe us, or care about us, we are to love them.

Does that mean we compromise the truth? Absolutely not. Does that mean we stop fighting for the unborn? No! We have to find a way to balance truth with love, and honesty with gentleness.

Question

9. Why is this balance so hard to achieve? What are some ways the pro-life community does well? What are some ways we could improve? How can we apply these truths to become more courageously pro-life?

   _____
   _____
   _____
   _____

CONCLUSION

God has called you to be a part of this. Your job is to educate, motivate, and inspire those around you. Part of that is caring for each and every person you meet and showing them what being pro-life really means.

NOTES

Week Ten

Equipping the Next Generation: Talking to Children and Teens

Introduction

A vital part of embracing our pro-life beliefs is passing them along to the next generation. Our children will not become pro-life just because we are; we have to teach them. We are up against a society that teaches them that abortion is okay, or that it's a personal decision. It's up to us as parents to intentionally teach our children about the inherent value of human life.

Related Scripture

Proverbs 22:6

Train up a child in the way he should go; even when he is old he will not depart from it.

Unfortunately, this is not the guarantee it is often made out to be! We all know families that did a great job parenting and had children turn away from God, and we know parents that did a terrible job and their children turned out wonderfully. Nonetheless, it is true that if we teach our children the right way to live, most of the time they will stick with it. They may depart for a time, but they will come back. Teaching our children is an incredibly important part of our responsibility as parents, and, unfortunately, one that is often neglected.

Deuteronomy 6:5–9

Teach your children all the time, and teach them from the very beginning. It is never too early to start talking with them about the things of God.

You shall love the LORD your God with all your heart and with all your soul and with all your might. And these words that I command you today shall be on your heart. You shall teach them diligently to your children, and shall talk of them when you sit in your house, and when you walk by the way, and when you lie down, and when you rise. You shall bind them as a sign on your hand, and they shall be as frontlets between your eyes. You shall write them on the doorposts of your house and on your gates.

When are we supposed to teach our children? All the time. When we sit at home, when we go places, when we go to bed, and when we wake up. We are to teach our children the words of God at every opportunity.

Question

1. What is it about our society that makes it difficult to follow the Biblical instructions for parents found in Proverbs 22:6 and Deuteronomy 6:5–9? What about our society helps?

_____
_____
_____
_____

Philippians 4:8

Finally, brothers, whatever is true, whatever is honorable, whatever is just, whatever is pure, whatever is lovely, whatever is commendable, if there is any excellence, if there is anything worthy of praise, think about these things.

We need to reflect on Philippians 4:8 as we teach our children. What should we focus on, negative things or positive things? Let me share a personal story. As I was doing research for this curriculum, I found myself reading, watching, and listening to a lot of material on suicide, abortion, and euthanasia. I watched popular TV shows and read books written by people with very anti-life viewpoints. As I was absorbing these things, I began to feel depressed. What was the point? Could we fight any of this? Is there any reason to try? If this material affected me, a mature Christian, this deeply, I can't imagine what it must do to our children.

Week Ten:
Equipping the Next Generation: Talking to Children and Teens

Our children need us to protect them. We want them to be able to deal with tough topics, but they need to be able to do so with the guidance and love of their parents. A parent's job is to guide and nurture their children until they're mature enough to make their own decisions. It's necessary to set boundaries and standards and tell them there are things they may not watch or listen to. Encourage your child to think on positive things and surround themselves with positive influences. If you find your child disconnecting or feeling depressed, find out what media is influencing them. What's on their phone? Their other devices? You're the parent. It is your job to intervene and make the unpopular choice to remove any media that is a destructive influence.

Question

2. How can balancing a child's freedom and safety be a challenge? At what age does this become difficult to deal with?

___

___

___

___

When Do We Start Teaching Our Children?

These life topics can be difficult to approach. However, if we're going to help our children cope with the world they live in, we need to address these issues before they arise in their lives.

These topics should be covered as soon as our children can interact and understand us. If we sit our children down to have one big talk about abortion, it's going to be awkward and probably unhelpful. However, if we teach our children about the value of human life from day one, it will help them approach these difficult subjects from a Christian viewpoint.

Question

3. What is the most challenging thing about approaching these topics with your kids? What makes it hard to bring them up? What might help?

___

___

___

___

Below are some suggestions for working with children of different ages. Each child is an individual, and you as a parent know what's best for yours. While it can be tempting to ignore or delay discussing pro-life topics, we must understand that our children need to hear about these difficult issues from us, their parents.

Age 0–5

- **Purchase and read pro-life children's books**
  - *Justice Loves Babies* by Danielle Wibeto
  - *Horton Hears a Who* by Dr. Seuss
  - *God Gave Us You* by Lisa Tawn Bergren
  - *You Are Special* by Max Lucado
- **Involve them in the pregnancy of family/friends**
  - Let them hear an unborn child's heartbeat and/or see an ultrasound image.
  - Make the unborn child a part of the family. Encourage them to talk to and interact with the unborn child.
  - Make sure they understand the baby is the same person before they're born as they are after they're born.
  - Show them ultrasound images of themselves before they were born and talk about how God created them.
- **Introduce them to pro-life activities**
  - Take them to a local pro-life event. Many are family-friendly (such as your local pregnancy center's Walk for Life).
  - Take them to the annual National March for Life.
  - Involve them in giving to a pro-life organization. Talk to them about helping babies and mothers.

Age 6–12

- **Continue reading—use discretion based on your child's maturity level**
  - Some children may need to stick with picture books and books that focus on valuing others. Other children may be ready to read young adult books.
- **Explain what abortion is**
  - Very simply explain that abortion is when a doctor ends a pregnancy before the child is ready to be born. You don't need to be graphic. If they ask questions, respond honestly and simply.
  - Explain fetal development more thoroughly. Talk about when unborn babies can hear/taste/smell.
  - Share with them that abortion is wrong and that it's our job to protect mothers and children.

- **Involve them in the pregnancy of family/friends**
  - Let them hear an unborn child's heartbeat and/or see an ultrasound scan.
  - Make the unborn child a part of the family. Involve them in shopping and planning for the new baby.
- **Continue pro-life activities**
  - Take them to local pro-life events.
  - Take them to the annual National March for Life. Many young teens attend these events, and your child will see that being pro-life is not just for old people!
  - Involve them in giving to a pro-life organization. Take them on a tour of a local pregnancy center. If they want to, let them use their money to purchase items for mothers and families in need.

Age 13–18

- **Make pro-life books available to them**
  - *The Giver* by Lois Lowry
  - *A Perfect Persecution* by James R. Lucas
  - *Abortion Rites* by Marvin Olasky
  - *Why Pro-Life?* by Randy Alcorn
  - *Third Time Around* by George Grant
  - *The Atonement Child* by Francine Rivers
  - *Matched* by Ally Condie

There are many pro-life books available for teens and adults. Encourage your teen to ask tough questions and commit to helping them find good answers.

- **Encourage abstinence**
  - Teach them to value themselves and their future marriage through abstinence.
  - Tell them you will love them *no matter what,* and encourage them to come to you with anything. Are they being offered drugs? Alcohol? Is an older person pursuing them? These types of problems thrive on secrecy. The more comfortable your teen is with you, the more likely they will be to talk to you when tough topics arise.
- **Show them young people participating in pro-life activities**
  - Check out the organization Students for Life and see if there is a chapter near you. Your teen or young adult child may not be interested, but it is good for them to see that there are many pro-life young people across the nation.
  - Take them to the National March for Life in Washington, DC.

All Ages

- **Involve them in pro-life work**
  - Take them to an event like Life Chain. Life Chain is a peaceful protest that happens annually across the nation where pro-life people gather in areas of high visibility and hold signs with positive pro-life messages.
  - Take them on a tour of your local pregnancy center.
  - Do a family workday at a local pro-life ministry.
  - Make a donation to a pro-life organization and talk about it!
  - Participate as a family in a pregnancy center's Walk for Life or other fundraiser.
- **Live it out**
  - Value everyone, even those that are unlovable. Love them like Jesus does.
  - Help people with disabilities and visit the elderly.
  - Don't have "the talk." Make being pro-life a fundamental part of your life, not a serious discussion you have once or twice.
  - If abortion or euthanasia come up in the news, help your children process the stories in the light of Biblical truth.

Question

4. What on this list seems most helpful? What is least helpful? What would you add to this list?

_____
_____
_____
_____

WHAT IF MY CHILD GETS PREGNANT?

We can get used to the idea of talking to our children about being pro-life, but often we can't imagine them in a situation where they would have to act upon their pro-life beliefs. Sure, they could help someone else, but they wouldn't experience an unplanned pregnancy of their own!

Christian kids who should know better make poor decisions all the time. It's part of growing up and having a brain that is still developing, especially the part of the brain where choices and risks are evaluated. How do we help our kids face decisions about sex or deal with an unplanned pregnancy?

- Encourage abstinence until marriage. Whether or not that was a choice you made for yourself, it's the best choice for your child. Set expectations for things like dating age and appropriate behavior with the opposite sex (1 Corinthians 6:13; Hebrews 13:4; 1 Thessalonians 4:3).
- Don't say you want them to abstain and then offer them birth control, allow them to attend questionable parties, or allow them to spend the night with someone of the opposite sex. Teens can only handle so much temptation, and it's the parent's job to keep their children safe. Don't send mixed messages.
- Assure your child that you love them no matter what and remind them that they can always come to you for help, comfort, and guidance. Don't tell them, "If you get pregnant, I'll throw you out of the house." They'll believe you and may get an abortion because they're afraid of telling you they made a poor decision.
- Do the right thing. If your child comes to you and tells you she's pregnant (or that his girlfriend is pregnant), it's up to you to help them choose life. It can be tempting to help them procure an abortion because you're afraid your child's life will be ruined. Realize that an abortion won't help them—it will only hurt them. You're the parent, and you need to help them make the right decision.
- Don't participate in your child's abortion. If your child, at any age, insists they need an abortion, you should not take part or pay for it. Should you love them anyway? Yes. Should you be there for them afterward? Absolutely. Should you drive them to the clinic, let them use your insurance, or give them cash? No. Offer good, life-affirming options no matter what.

Question

5. How would you handle this situation? What would be the right way to approach a child's/grandchild's pregnancy? What would be the wrong way to approach it? If someone in your family was treated poorly because of a pregnancy, what should you do about it?

_____
_____
_____
_____

What Are Our Children Up Against?

Our culture is full of technology that previous generations did not have. Technology is a blessing in many ways, but it can be a burden, especially to our children. Bullying can follow them into the home. Graphic content can be viewed in the privacy of their bedrooms. Parents often can't keep up with what their children are viewing and aren't aware of what sorts of issues they should be addressing.

What are your kids watching? Make sure you know. Keep an eye on their viewing habits. It only takes a moment and an accidental click for your child to be exposed to something harmful and/or disturbing.

What can we do?

- Talk to your children. Listen to what they have to say. They'll tell you more than you think they will.
- Monitor their activity, especially on their mobile devices. It's not about whether or not you trust your child. It's about understanding that there is a world of temptation and hurt out there that you don't want them exposed to. Keep up to date with what apps are available and which ones are a risk for your child.
- Be the parent. If you find out your child has been viewing porn, taking or viewing inappropriate photos, talking to older members of the opposite sex, or shopping for inappropriate items, take drastic measures. Your child won't like it, but it's your responsibility to keep them safe.
- Make sure your children understand your values and why you hold them. They shouldn't find themselves in a compromising situation wondering what you would want them to do. Talk about situations they may encounter so they know how to make the right decision. Set up code words or phrases they can use to let you know they're in trouble without being obvious about it.
- Assure them that you love them no matter what and they can always call you for help. There may be appropriate consequences, but if they're in bad place, they should be able to call you without fear.
- If they want to watch, listen to, or read something you find objectionable, consider whether there is value in walking through it with them. Certainly, some things should be avoided, but there are others that can provide excellent teaching opportunities.
- Be intentional when it comes to teaching your children. Your attitude and lifestyle will have a significant impact, but don't underestimate the power of your words.

Question

6. What are our children dealing with today? What are some examples of media that could be negatively influencing them?

_____
_____
_____
_____

Week Ten:
Equipping the Next Generation: Talking to Children and Teens

My Children Are Young Adults—They Won't Listen to Me!

Reaching adult children can be tough. They don't know everything, but they're sure they can't learn anything from you. What is your role with children you can no longer require obedience from? Know that if your children are still living in your home (regardless of their age) or they are dependent on you financially, you have authority in their lives. They may not like it, and it may be uncomfortable for you, but you can (and should!) expect certain behaviors from them. If you're paying for the WiFi, you are in control of what comes into your house. If you're paying the electric bill, you get to say what can and cannot be viewed on TV and other devices. If you're supporting a child, in full or in part, you can insist they attend church or follow other rules (such as not engaging in premarital sex or hosting wild parties in the home/dorm you pay for).

If they're living independently it is more difficult, but you can still be the loving voice of truth in their lives. More than that, you can pray for them and for the decisions they're making. If your relationship does not permit even gentle, loving correction, you can still intercede for them in prayer. Be careful how you pray; focus on asking for God's will and truth in their lives. Asking for material blessings for a disobedient and willful child will likely not guide them back into the fold. Sometimes God's direction can seem harsh and unloving to us, but it is often the best thing for them. Encourage positive behavior as much as you can and pray for them faithfully.

We Don't Have Time!

Do you want to educate your children but don't have time? Life can often be hectic. You get everyone up in the morning and rush out the door to work and school. By the time everyone gets home, dinner is eaten, and homework is done, you're exhausted and ready for bed. Not to mention household chores, children with sports and after-school activities, and social lives that make everyone busier.

Sometimes there is nothing you can do about your schedule. Maybe you're a single parent barely making ends meet. Perhaps you have a special-needs child or a disabled spouse. If you truly can't make as much time as you need, here are some ideas:

- Enlist help. Find someone in your church willing to invest in your child's life. Someone you can trust to care for your child and offer good advice. Perhaps this person is childless or has grown children—this could be an amazing ministry opportunity for them.

- Make the most of the time you do have. Schedule one night or morning every week that is nonnegotiable family time. You don't have to spend this time lecturing your children, rather let it be time spent learning about one another and listening. You will have many educational opportunities simply by asking your children what's going on and responding.
- Hire out. You have to work, but can you hire housekeeping help to take some of the pressure off? Can you do pizza one night a week? Find a way to spend dedicated time with your children. Even if it doesn't seem like much, it will make a difference.

Teaching our children can be difficult, but it's part of our God-given responsibility as parents. Whether or not you have children in your home, you certainly have a child or two in your life. You can be a positive influence on these children if you look for opportunities.

Question

7. Examine your life and the lives of those in your family. How can you make time to educate your children? Are there extra activities that can be cut out? If this isn't your stage of life, what can you do to help others who are struggling?

_____
_____
_____
_____

Conclusion

Equipping our children to accurately and passionately defend their beliefs is a key part of parenting. Remember, childhood is not a state people can live in forever. Our children must be raised to be self-sufficient, mature, and reasoning adults. Teaching them to understand their faith will have a longer-lasting impact on their lives than their athletic ability or extracurricular activities.

NOTES

WEEK ELEVEN

Part One: Where Do We Go From Here? Individual Responsibility

Introduction

For the past ten weeks we have learned about some of the challenges plaguing society today, and we've discussed what our responsibilities are. But what exactly do we do about it? It can be frustrating when someone tells you about a great need but doesn't give you concrete steps to take to fill that need. For the next two weeks we'll discuss where to go from here and figure out where we fit in. This is not just about us as individuals; this is also about us as a church, a community, and a nation.

Related Scripture

Luke 8:42b–55

As Jesus went, the people pressed around him. And there was a woman who had had a discharge of blood for twelve years, and though she had spent all her living on physicians, she could not be healed by anyone. She came up behind him and touched the fringe of his garment, and immediately her discharge of blood ceased. And Jesus said, "Who was it that touched me?" When all denied it, Peter said, "Master, the crowds surround you and are pressing in on you!" But Jesus said, "Someone touched me, for I perceive that power has gone out from me." And when the woman saw that she was not hidden, she came trembling, and falling down before him declared in the presence of all the people why she had touched him, and how she had been immediately healed. And he said to her, "Daughter, your faith has made you well; go in peace."

Week Eleven: Part One:
Where Do We Go From Here? Individual Responsibility

While he was still speaking, someone from the ruler's house came and said, "Your daughter is dead; do not trouble the Teacher anymore." But Jesus on hearing this answered him, "Do not fear; only believe, and she will be well." And when he came to the house, he allowed no one to enter with him, except Peter and John and James, and the father and mother of the child. And all were weeping and mourning for her, but he said, "Do not weep, for she is not dead but sleeping." And they laughed at him, knowing that she was dead. But taking her by the hand he called, saying, "Child, arise." And her spirit returned, and she got up at once. And he directed that something should be given her to eat.

Jesus ministered to two sick women, one who was probably older and had likely been aged by her disease, and another who was very young. The first would have been kept separate from the rest of the Israelites—she wasn't even supposed to touch anyone (Leviticus 15:25–27). The second was the daughter of a leader in the synagogue; someone, the world would say, Jesus should pay attention to. He did, but first He stopped to help this poor, desperate, broken woman. She had nowhere else to turn, and He was there for her.

Questions

1. How do we respond to those who are sick? Are they fun to be around? Is it awkward? Do we avoid them?

   _____
   _____
   _____
   _____

2. What is our individual responsibility toward those who are hurting and broken? What are we called to do? How can we make a difference?

   _____
   _____
   _____
   _____

Matthew 19:13–15

Then children were brought to him that he might lay his hands on them and pray. The disciples rebuked the people, but Jesus said, "Let the little children come to me and do not hinder them, for to such belongs the kingdom of heaven." And he laid his hands on them and went away.

In this passage, Jesus ministered to little children. Do you picture happy, smiling, chubby babies and toddlers clustered around Him, sitting quietly on His knee as he lays His hands on them? Clearly, you have not been around small children!

Kids are messy, love them anyway!

Try to forget the flannelgraphs of your youth and think about *actual* children. Not just children, but children before the invention of baby wipes or disposable diapers. Children born into varying levels of poverty in an oppressed nation that was essentially a giant sandbox. Someone had his finger in his nose, another had a soggy diaper, one was making interesting noises in his pants, and at least three were crying. But you know what? Jesus loved them. He touched them. He let them touch Him (without the benefit of being able to stuff His robe in the washing machine later!). Their mothers couldn't take them to a state-of-the-art emergency room if they got sick, but they could take them to the Prophet to be blessed.

In our culture, a common reason given for helping others is that it makes us feel good. Is that enough reason to help someone? Sure, sometimes it does make us feel good—but what about when it doesn't? What then?

Truly caring for others can make us feel uncomfortable. Being genuinely pro-life is about caring for others despite being uncomfortable. It's about feeling awkward, not knowing what to say and not knowing what to do. It's about relying on the Holy Spirit to guide us and give us His love.

Question

3. When was the last time caring for someone made you feel uncomfortable or cost you something? How does this conform with the idea that helping others should make us feel good?

_____
_____
_____
_____

Hebrews 10:24–25

And let us consider how to stir up one another to love and good works, not neglecting to meet together, as is the habit of some, but encouraging one another, and all the more as you see the Day drawing near.

We have a personal responsibility to encourage others. Part of that encouragement is holding others accountable and part of it is encouraging one another to do good works. If you see a fellow believer neglecting their spiritual life or the spiritual lives of their children, it's okay to call them out on it. It's okay to ask others what they did for the cause of life this week—just don't get mad if they ask you the same question!

Question

4. How do you feel about holding others accountable? What about letting others hold you accountable? What are some other ways we can encourage others?

___

"You're Just Pro-Birth!"

Have you heard the phrase, "You're just pro-birth?" Somehow pro-lifers have been reduced to being people who only want babies to be born and have no interest in them after that. This is where personal experience comes in handy. When it comes to helping needy families, what do you do? What do the organizations you support do for those in need? It's possible the people around you (and hopefully you as well) are showing that they're pro-all-life, not just pro-unborn baby.

Don't brush off this accusation and move on. The pro-choice movement has a point. There are plenty of people who insist that abortion should be illegal but have little interest in caring for the children after they have been born. This is a good time to examine yourself and ask, "Am I pro-life, or am I just pro-birth?" Being pro-life is not just about wanting babies to be born; it's about committing ourselves to caring for and supporting them for the long haul.

Interestingly, in many ways it is much easier to be pro-choice than it is to be pro-life. Being pro-choice requires little more of someone than voting to ensure abortionists have free rein and plenty of tax money. Being truly pro-life is much more difficult *and* much more rewarding.

What are some ways we can be truly and courageously pro-life?

- Fostering and adoption. This is HUGE! There are many children languishing in foster care that need someone to love and care for them. Do you have space in your house for a child? If an orphaned child knocked on your door, would you take them in? Consider this a knock. They need you!

- If fostering or adopting isn't something you can do, look into ways you can help families who are fostering or adopting. Can you help financially? Purchase items the kids need? Babysit? Make a meal? Run errands? Do dishes? Mow the lawn? Absorbing a new child, especially one with trauma in their past, is exhausting and unsettling. Whether or not they announce it, these families need our help.

This little one could have been stuck in foster care for years if a young couple hadn't decided to follow God's call to adopt. She now has a happy, healthy forever home with two loving parents!

- Help a single parent. Parenthood is demanding, and single parenting can be even more difficult. Do you know a single mom or dad? They could probably use your help. Get to know them and their kids and love on them. You can make a difference!
- Donate to a pro-life organization. They're everywhere and they need your help! I don't mean simply filling a baby bottle full of loose change—pray and ask God what sacrificial gift He is calling you to make. Trust me, in eternity it will be well worth it.
- Get to know your local pro-life leaders. What's their story? What makes them tick? What do they need? The more you know, the more you'll feel comfortable getting involved.
- Get involved with other ministries. Being pro-life means caring for people in all stages of life with allthe challenges that go along with them. Some babies saved from abortion end up being homeless, struggling with addiction, or dealing with poverty. They need you to step in and invest in their lives.
- Research the organizations you donate to. Are they truly pro-life? What are their values? Who is on their Board of Directors? Always do your research before putting your money into an organization.

Questions

5. Are you pro-life or are you pro-birth? What are some of your actions—not beliefs—that show you are truly pro-life?

_____
_____
_____
_____

6. Are you doing any of the suggestions listed above? Which one makes you the most uncomfortable? Why?

_____
_____
_____
_____

Week Eleven: Part One:
Where Do We Go From Here? Individual Responsibility

Discerning Our Personal Calling

We're all busy, right? Here's the question we have to ask ourselves: Are we busy because we're fulfilling God's calling on our lives, or are we busy because we like being busy? God knows that we're human and we're limited. He doesn't want us to burn out. He does, however, expect us to know His calling rather than jumping into any activity that sounds good. Are you called to adopt? If you are, fulfilling that calling means you can't do other things. Just because something is good or should be done doesn't mean you should be the one doing it. In fact, doing something just because it needs to be done could not only prevent you from fulfilling your calling, but it could prevent someone else from fulfilling theirs. Why would they volunteer if you're already doing it?

Prayerfully consider what God is calling you to do and what He *isn't* calling you to do. He tells us that His yoke is easy and His burden is light (Matthew 11:30). If you're feeling overburdened, perhaps you're taking on responsibilities that are not yours. That being said, don't worry about what your fellow church members, neighbors, or family members are doing. Focus on you and your calling (John 21:21–22).

At the same time, saying, "It's not my calling," can simply be an excuse. If you're ignoring the work God has called you to, you're missing out on helping others and being blessed for your obedience (either now or in eternity). Each of us is called to serve God and seek His kingdom.

Are you "too busy?" Sit down and take a look at what makes you busy. Write out a list with your spouse, family, or a friend. Which activities are part of God's calling on your life and which aren't? God will show you what He has for you if you ask and listen.

Group Discussion

What can we personally do to make a difference? How can we hold ourselves accountable? Make a list of concrete steps you're going to take and give yourselves a timeline. Keep your goals SMART! SMART stands for specific, measurable, achievable, relevant, and time-bound.[122] There are a myriad of online and print resources about setting goals. If you're not sure how to do it, do some research—your group will thank you!

Conclusion

It may seem overwhelming to take on a new project, goal, or charity to support. Spend time with God making sure your plans are His plans, then put your future in His hands and take a step of faith.

NOTES

WEEK TWELVE

Part Two: Where do we go from here? Church, Community, and National Responsibility

Introduction

Last week we talked about what we can do as individuals. As Americans, this is comfortable for us. We act, think, and behave as individuals. Sometimes we're okay in small groups of likeminded people, but we often struggle when thinking about ourselves as part of a larger group—especially one that doesn't always agree with us.

This week we're going to wrestle with the concepts of community and national responsibility and discuss what we can do in our churches, communities, and nation to make a difference.

Related Scripture

Jonah 4:10–11

And the Lord said, "You pity the plant, for which you did not labor, nor did you make it grow, which came into being in a night and perished in a night. And should not I pity Nineveh, that great city, in which there are more than 120,000 persons who do not know their right hand from their left, and also much cattle?"

In the Old Testament, God regularly dealt with idolatrous nations, and His judgments were often violent and painful. Have you ever stopped to think about the people in those nations? Were there any children swept up in the violence? What about the righteous few? Were they spared pain and destruction? We're probably all familiar with the story of how Jonah was called by God to preach repentance in Nineveh, went the opposite direction of where he was supposed to go, was swallowed by a great fish, spat out on dry land, and then finally did the work he was supposed to do in the first place. At the end of the account, God speaks to Jonah and says there are 120,000 people in the city of Nineveh (the capital of Assyria) that can't tell their right and left hands apart. What does that mean? There were 120,000 children.[1] Babies! Little ones who wouldn't have a clue about what was going on. We read in the book of Jonah that the city repented and God didn't destroy them (spoilers: it didn't last and they were destroyed later).[123] But what if He had struck down the city? Do you think the children or other vulnerable people would have been spared? No. We know that historically (and today) the vulnerable are destroyed as quickly, and often with more brutality, as the oppressors and decision-makers.

Questions

1. Is the possibility of Nineveh's destruction hard for you to think about? Why do we shy away from the idea that vulnerable people or victims of others' poor choices can be swept up in judgment? While Nineveh was spared, there are other examples of people groups who weren't. What does it mean for us today to know that God destroyed the vulnerable (Genesis 19; Joshua 6:21)?

   _____
   _____
   _____
   _____

2. Does God still judge cities and nations today? What about the final judgement? Could we be called out for being part of a nation that brutally murders over a million children every year (2 Corinthians 5:10; Romans 14:10; Revelation 20:11–15)?

   _____
   _____
   _____
   _____

---

[1] Some scholars believe that the 120,000 refers to the entire city, not just children. Either way, there would have been a lot of children involved. Try not to get hung up on the detail.

Week Twelve: Part Two:
Where do we go from here? Church, Community, and National Responsibility

2 Chronicles 7:14

If my people who are called by my name humble themselves, and pray and seek my face and turn from their wicked ways, then I will hear from heaven and will forgive their sin and heal their land.

Here is the good news: God has given us a formula (which the people of Nineveh successfully followed) to get ourselves out of trouble. We humble ourselves, we pray, and we turn from our wicked ways.

It is very important that we don't over-spiritualize this. We like to think that turning from our wicked ways is some super-spiritual exercise we perform by being alone in prayer and vowing to be a nicer person. Not quite. Turning from our wicked ways involves work. And it's not just our personal wicked ways we need to turn from; it encompasses the wicked ways of the nation we're a part of. Turning away could be actively working against sin by voting, volunteering in helping ministries, donating to organizations that make a difference, and making your voice heard. Any action that resists the sinfulness of our nation, in a godly way, is a practical way to turn our nation back to one that honors God.

Question

3. What does 2 Chronicles 7:14 tell us about our responsibility regarding the wickedness of our nation? How can we be part of turning our nation away from wickedness?

_____
_____
_____
_____

Matthew 6:25–33

"Therefore I tell you, do not be anxious about your life, what you will eat or what you will drink, nor about your body, what you will put on. Is not life more than food, and the body more than clothing? Look at the birds of the air: they neither sow nor reap nor gather into barns, and yet your heavenly Father feeds them. Are you not of more value than they? And which of you by being anxious can add a single hour to his span of life? And why are you anxious about clothing? Consider the lilies of the field, how they grow: they neither toil nor spin, yet I tell you, even Solomon in all his glory was not arrayed like one of these. But if God so clothes the grass of the field, which today is alive and tomorrow is thrown into the oven, will he not much more clothe you, O you of little faith? Therefore do not be anxious, saying, 'What shall we eat?' or 'What shall we drink?' or 'What shall we wear?' For the Gentiles seek after all these things,

and your heavenly Father knows that you need them all. But seek first the kingdom of God and his righteousness, and all these things will be added to you.

What does this have to do with our nation? Matthew 6:25–33 tells us what really matters—the kingdom of God. When we think about stepping out, making a difference, or sacrificially involving ourselves in something greater, what stops us?

Take fostering children, for example. What stops us from being foster or adoptive parents? Often, it's our desire for comfort. We don't want a stranger coming into our home. It's awkward, uncomfortable, and costly. It might not work out, and we might have to watch them go back into a bad situation. We don't want to sacrifice our desires in order to help someone else. Another example: What keeps us from financially supporting kingdom work? We have our needs and wants, so we pay for those first. Then, any money left over goes to God.

But what does Matthew 6:25–33 tell us? We're to seek *first* God's kingdom. Then, and only then, will these things be added to us. We're not supposed to focus on what we're going to eat or what we're going to wear (or, should I say, where we're going on vacation?). We're supposed to focus on God's kingdom.

Questions

4. Fostering and adopting abused, neglected, and orphaned children is just one example of acting out our pro-life convictions. But what keeps us from seeking God's kingdom first? How does anxiety about our lives prevent us from doing kingdom work?

   _____
   _____
   _____
   _____

5. How could Christians who are truly focused on kingdom work change the course of our nation? Has it happened before? Could it happen again?

   _____
   _____
   _____
   _____

Ephesians 6:12

For we do not wrestle against flesh and blood, but against the rulers, against the authorities, against the cosmic powers over this present darkness, against the spiritual forces of evil in the heavenly places.

Week Twelve: Part Two:
Where do we go from here? Church, Community, and National Responsibility

We can't fool ourselves into thinking this is a battle we can win on a purely physical plane. If we're talking about taking our nation back for life, we have to acknowledge that we're fighting a spiritual battle. Every mother that chooses abortion destroys a part of herself, and many start a downward slide into grief, depression, and even addiction.[124] Every family that kills its own children starts to break apart. Families are the cornerstone on which society is built, and the family unit, in part through abortion, is under attack. So, yes, our battle is individual, but it is also national.

Question

6. What's your opinion of spiritual warfare as discussed in Ephesians 6:12? Do you think we need to be aware of this?

___

John 16:33

I have said these things to you, that in me you may have peace. In the world you will have tribulation. But take heart; I have overcome the world.

Christ tells us to expect bad things to happen. This can cause us to feel disheartened, overwhelmed, and discouraged. But you know what? Christ has overcome the world! He has already won, and through Him we will win too. Commit yourself to doing God's will and living out His plan. He knows what needs to be done, and He will help you find your role.

It's never too early or too late to get on board. Whether you're twelve or one hundred years old, God has things for you to do. Ask Him—He will show you. You may have to change, and you will probably feel uncomfortable, but He *will* show you!

Question

7. What does "I have overcome the world" in John 16:33 mean to you? How does it make you feel?

___

We the People

The first Sunday school class that used this curriculum wrestled mightily with the topic of national responsibility. Russell Ponziani, one of the participants, shared this with us:

As Americans, we're responsible for what our government does. Whether we agree or not, it's on us.

Not since God put a king in Israel have the people of a nation been so accountable. "We the People" are in charge. Our country is designed so that the individual is responsible for what the government does. "We the People" have individual freedom, therefore we have individual accountability. We elect the people to represent our values. If our values are more for our pocketbook then for the lives of children, you get what we have now. The majority of Americans don't support abortion. We have the moral and Constitutional authority to stop it, but we don't make it a priority. Abortion is not a Republican/Democrat issue, abortion is a "We the People" issue. I vote pro-life and give of my time and money to pro-life causes, yet the blood is on my hands because I am "We the People."

Whether or not we personally support abortion, we are responsible for the choices of our nation. We have power over what our government does, yet for forty-five years we have allowed murder to be legal, turning a blind eye toward this transgression. God is just, He cannot and will not ignore the brutal murder of millions of unborn children.

Christians Can Change the World

The history lessons of the earlier part of our study show us how Christians from all walks of life can make a difference. Whether we're lawmakers, social workers, businesspeople, pastors, parents, mechanics, farmers, accountants, or serving fast food, we work together to help those who are most in need. Fighting against sin isn't a one-and-done proposition. However, every time we affect one person, born or unborn, we change the world.

Week Twelve: Part Two:
Where do we go from here? Church, Community, and National Responsibility

Question

8. Why does sin often seem so overwhelming? Why does the magnitude of sin make us want to throw our hands in the air and give up? How can we fight this tendency? How can we change our culture?

_____
_____
_____
_____

What Do We Do?

This series isn't just about us becoming better advocates or achieving a better understanding of what it means to be pro-life. It's about working together to heal our nation. In 2 Chronicles 7:14, God says His people must "humble themselves, and pray and seek my face and turn from their wicked ways." There is hope. This fight for life is not over. Each and every one of us can make a difference. Eventually the tide will turn, and we will become a nation that values life.

How do we shift the course of our nation?

- Vote. Once again, this seems simple, but this is an excellent way to make our voices heard.
- Serve in public office. Yuck, politics, right? But someone has to do it, and we need Christians to vote for!
- Educate our children. The hand that rocks the cradle is the hand that rules the world.[125] Make sure you're teaching your children and grandchildren the ways of the Lord.
- Educate our churches. Don't let this curriculum be the first and last thing your church does about abortion. Keep the conversation going.
- Give to and get involved with local and national pro-life organizations. There are people who are working themselves into the ground to save lives—they need your help!
- Pray. This may seem obvious, but pray for our nation, our churches, our leaders, our children, and those who are working to save the unborn. Prayer works!

Question

9. Which of these suggestions, or others, seems to be the most difficult? Which is the easiest?

_____
_____
_____
_____

What Is Already Happening?

There is no need to reinvent the wheel. There are plenty of organizations already doing great work. All you have to do is step up and get involved. The half-dozen places listed below are just a fraction of the groups doing vital pro-life work in our nation.

- Local Pro-Life Pregnancy Help Organizations (PHOs). These places—pregnancy centers, maternity homes, and adoption agencies—are the "soft underbelly" of the pro-life movement. They're expensive to maintain and they're vulnerable to the more militant members of the pro-choice community. Find your local organization and get involved. Give, pray, or volunteer, but don't underestimate how much they need the help of churches and individuals. The national groups are called Heartbeat International and Care Net—they can help you find your local PHOs if you aren't sure who they are.
- Heartbeat International, NIFLA, and CareNet. These three organizations work to support and educate pregnancy centers worldwide. They need financial support as well as volunteer help.
- National Right to Life state and local chapters. This organization and its offshoots are dedicated to changing our country. Get in touch with your local group and see what they need.
- March for Life. This is not simply a once-a-year event: this is an organization. Whether or not you can attend the national march in Washington, DC, you can be supportive.
- Students for Life. This group works with high school and college students, helping to educate and mobilize young people to make a difference.
- 40 Days for Life. They make concentrated prayer efforts outside of abortion clinics. If you're looking to get involved in some serious prayer, they can help!
- Rachel's Vineyard. This is a group that helps women heal after an abortion. If this is where your heart lies, you can help support other women as they go

through their healing journey. (Many PHOs also have post-abortive healing programs.)
- And Then There Were None. This group helps abortion workers exit the abortion industry. This is a great way to end abortion!

Group Discussion

What can we do, as a group, to make a difference? How can we hold our group accountable? If there isn't one already, how can we start a pro-life group in our church? Take time this week to discuss concrete steps you can take as a church body to make a difference in your community. No matter where you are, there are things you can do to be more courageously pro-life. Don't let this week's class end without an action plan!

Conclusion

God is calling us to get involved. As a community, we need to determine exactly what He is asking us to do. Abortion and euthanasia are so terrible and sinful that we are all required to take part in eradicating them from our world.

Being courageously pro-life is part of being a Christian. There is no other choice for us. To neglect our holy responsibility of protecting the weakest among us is to shirk our God-given duty. The question isn't, "Should I get involved?" The question is, "What does God want me to do?"

Don't forget what you have learned over the past twelve weeks. Allow it to sink into your heart and make it a part of you. Let it radically change how you approach the world. You and your church can be part of transforming our nation into one that embraces and embodies a culture of life.

NOTES

Appendix

Abortion Laws by State

The next four pages are a summary of abortion laws in each state. Please be aware that the landscape is constantly shifting, and while this table is correct as of May 2019, it could have changed. To obtain an up-to-date chart, go to the Guttmacher Institute's website and search for "current abortion law."

Please be aware that the Guttmacher Institute is a pro-choice institute, and the language they use reflects that stance.[126]

Overview of Abortion Laws by State Source Page 1 of 4: guttmacher.org

State	Must be performed by a licensed physician.	Must be performed in a hospital if at this stage.	Second physician must participate if at this stage.	Prohibited except in cases of life or health endangerment if at this stage.	"Partial-Birth" Abortion is banned.	Public Funding of Abortion		Private insurance coverage is limited.
						Funds all or most medically necessary abortions.	Funds limited to life endangerment, rape, and incest.	
AL		Viability	Viability	20 wks*	▼		X	
AK	X				▼	X		
AZ	X	Viability	Viability	Viability	X	X		X
AR	X		Viability	20 wks†	X		X	
CA				Viability		X		
CO							X	
CT		Viability		Viability		X		
DE	X			Viability$^\Omega$			X	
DC							X	
FL	X	Viability	24 wks	24 wks	▼		X	
GA	X			20 wks*	Post-viability		X	
HI	X$^\xi$			Viability		X		
ID	X	Viability	3rd tri.	Viability	▼		X	X
IL	X$^\xi$		Viability	Viability	▼	X		
IN	X	20 wks	20 wks	20 wks*	X		X*	X
IA	X			20 wks*	▼		X	
KS	X		Viability	20 wks*	X		X	X

wks = weeks   tri = trimester

▼	Permanently enjoined; law not in effect.
*	Exception in case of threat to the woman's physical health.
†	Exception in case of rape or incest.
‡	Exception in case of life endangerment only. A 2016 New York Attorney General opinion determined that the state's law conflicts with U.S. Supreme Court rulings on abortion, and that abortion care is permissible under the U.S. Constitution to protect a woman's health, or when the fetus is not viable.
Ω	Exception in case of fetal abnormality.
ξ	Only applies to surgical abortion. In New Mexico, some but not all advanced practice clinicians may provide medication abortion.
Φ	Law limits abortion provision to OB/GYNs.

Overview of Abortion Laws by State Source Page 2 of 4: guttmacher.org							
State	Must be performed by a licensed physician.	Must be performed in a hospital if at this stage.	Second physician must participate if at this stage.	Prohibited except in cases of life or health endangerment if at this stage.	"Partial-Birth" Abortion is banned.	Public Funding of Abortion		Private insurance coverage is limited.
						Funds all or most medically necessary abortions.	Funds limited to life endangerment, rape, and incest.	
KY	X	2nd tri.		20 wks*	▼		X	X
LA	X		Viability	20 wks*	X		X	
ME	X			Viability			X	
MD	X			Viability$^\Omega$		X		
MA	X$^\xi$			24 wks		X		
MI	X			Viability‡	X		X	X
MN	X		20 wks	Viability		X		
MS	X$^\Phi$			20 wks*$^\epsilon$	X		X$^\Omega$	
MO	X	Viability	Viability	Viability	▼		X	X
MT			Viability	Viability*	Post-viability	X		
NE	X			20 wks*	▼		X	X
NV	X	24 wks		24 wks			X	
NH					X		X	
NJ	X$^\xi$	14 wks			▼	X		
NM	X$^\xi$				Post-viability	X		
NY	X$^\xi$		24 wks	24 wks‡		X		
NC	X	20 wks		20 wks			X	
ND	X			20 wks*	X		X	X
OH	X	20 wks	20 wks	20 wks*	X		X	
OK	X	2nd tri	Viability	20 wks*	X		X	X
OR						X		
PA	X	Viability	Viability	24 wks*			X	
RI	X$^\xi$			24 wks‡	▼		X	▼
SC	X	3rd tri	3rd tri	20 wks*	X		X	
SD	X	24 wks		20 wks*	X		Life Only	
TN	X	Viability	Viability	Viability*	X		X	
TX	X			20 wks*	X		X	
UT	X			Viability$^{\dagger\Omega}$	X		X*	X
VT						X	X$^\Omega$	
VA	X	2nd tri	Viability	3rd tri	X		X$^\Omega$	
WA	X$^\xi$			Viability		X		
WV				20 wks*	▼		X*$^\Omega$	
WI	X	Viability		20 wks*	▼		X*	
WY	X			Viability			X	
TOTAL	42	19	19	43	20	16	33+DC	11

wks = weeks   tri = trimester

▼	Permanently enjoined; law not in effect.
*	Exception in case of threat to the woman's physical health.
†	Exception in case of rape or incest.
‡	Exception in case of life endangerment only. A 2016 New York Attorney General opinion determined that the state's law conflicts with U.S. Supreme Court rulings on abortion, and that abortion care is permissible under the U.S. Constitution to protect a woman's health, or when the fetus is not viable.
Ω	Exception in case of fetal abnormality.
ξ	Only applies to surgical abortion. In New Mexico, some but not all advanced practice clinicians may provide medication abortion.
Φ	Law limits abortion provision to OB/GYNs.
€	A court has temporarily blocked enforcement of a Mississippi law that would have banned abortion at 15 weeks after the patient's last menstrual period.

Overview of Abortion Laws by State: Page 3 of 4 Source: guttmacher.org						
State	Providers may refuse to participate.		Mandated counseling includes:			Waiting period after counseling (in hours):	Parental involvement required for minors.
	Individual	Institution	Breast Cancer Link	Fetal Pain	Negative Psychological Effects		
AL						48	Consent
AK	X	Private	X	X			▼
AZ	X	X				24	Consent
AR	X	X		X$^\Phi$		48	Consent
CA	X	Religious					▼
CO							Notice
CT	X						
DE	X	X					Notice$^\xi$
DC							
FL	X	X				▼	Notice
GA	X	X		X		24	Notice
HI	X	X					
ID	X	X				24	Consent
IL	X	Private					Notice
IN	X	Private		X		18	Consent
IA	X	Private				§	Notice
KS	X	X	X	X	X	24	Consent
KY	X	X				24	Consent
LA	X	X		X	X	24	Consent
ME	X	X					
MD	X	X					Notice
MA	X	X				▼	Consent
MI	X	X			X	24	Consent
MN	X	Private		X$^\Phi$		24	Notice þ
MS	X	X	X			24	Consent þ
MO	X	X		X$^\Phi$		72	Consent
MT	X	Private				▼	▼
NE	X	X			X	24	Consent
NV	X	Private					▼

▼	Permanently enjoined; law not in effect.
§	Enforcement temporarily enjoined by court order; policy not in effect.
Φ	Fetal pain information is given only to women who are at least 20 weeks gestation; in Missouri at 22 weeks gestation.
þ	Both parents must consent to the abortion.
ξ	Specified health professionals may waive parental involvement in certain circumstances.
◊	In South Dakota, the waiting period excludes weekends or annual holidays and in Utah the waiting period is waived in cases of rape, incest, fetal defect or if the patient is younger than 15.

Overview of Abortion Laws by State: Page 4 of 4 Source: guttmacher.org						
−State	Providers may refuse to participate.		Mandated counseling includes:			Waiting period after counseling (in hours):	Parental involvement required for minors.
	Individual	Institution	Breast Cancer Link	Fetal Pain	Negative Psychological Effects		
NH							Notice
NJ	X	Private					▼
NM	X	X					▼
NY	X						
NC	X	X			X	72	Consent
ND	X	X				24	Consent[þ]
OH	X	X				24	Consent
OK	X	Private	X	X[Φ]		72	Consent & Notice
OR	X	Private					
PA	X	Private				24	Consent
RI	X						Consent
SC	X	Private				24	Consent
SD	X	X		X	X	72[◊]	Notice
TN	X	X				48	Consent
TX	X	Private	X	X	X	24	Consent & Notice
UT	X	Private		X[Φ]		72[◊]	Consent & Notice
VT							
VA	X	X				24	Consent & Notice
WA	X	X					
WV					X	24	Notice[ξ]
WI	X	X		X		24	Consent[ξ]
WY	X	Private					Consent & Notice
TOTAL	45	42	5	13	8	27	37

▼	Permanently enjoined; law not in effect.
§	Enforcement temporarily enjoined by court order; policy not in effect.
Φ	Fetal pain information is given only to women who are at least 20 weeks gestation; in Missouri at 22 weeks gestation.
þ	Both parents must consent to the abortion.
ξ	Specified health professionals may waive parental involvement in certain circumstances.
◊	In South Dakota, the waiting period excludes weekends or annual holidays and in Utah the waiting period is waived in cases of rape, incest, fetal defect or if the patient is younger than 15.

Post-Abortive Healing Resources

Have you had an abortion or have you been involved in an abortion? Does this decision weigh you down or affect you in other ways? There is hope! The Bible tells us that Christ forgives all sins (1 John 1:9), including abortion.

Even knowing that Christ forgives, there can still be mental and emotional damage resulting from an abortion. There are many healing resources available (listed below).

Post-Abortive Healing Resources

1. Rachel's Vineyard – http://www.rachelsvineyard.org/
2. Abortion Recovery International – http://www.abortionrecoveryinternational.org/
3. Concepts of Truth International – www.internationalhelpline.org
4. Or, contact your local Pregnancy Medical Center. They may be aware of local groups that are not listed here.

Confidential Self-Assessment

1. I have had an abortion in my past. yes / no

2. If yes, I have been through a healing program for that abortion. yes / no

   If you answered "yes" to question 1 and "no" to question 2, I (Sarah) strongly recommend you seek healing before continuing this class. Abortion is a very painful experience and the topics explored here can bring up pain from your past. If you answered "yes" to question 1 & 2, I would recommend sharing this with your teacher or someone you trust in the class.

3. I have participated in an abortion in the past (as a friend, father, grandparent, sister, etc). yes / no

4. If yes, I have dealt with this past abortion and experienced healing and forgiveness. yes / no

   If you said "yes" to question 3 and "no" to question 4, you may want to consider seeking healing before participating in this class. People react very differently to being part of an abortion experience that was not their own.

5. I struggle with anger toward women who have had abortions. yes / no

   If yes, take some time to take this to the Lord in prayer. If He has forgiven someone, or is willing to forgive someone, then you have no right to remain angry with them.

6. I am pro-choice—I don't see why abortion is such a big deal. yes / no

   That's OK! Please attend anyway with an open mind and heart.

7. I am pro-life, but I think abortion is OK in certain cases. It isn't for me to judge. yes / no

   Please keep your heart and mind open to new ideas.

8. I am very pro-life, but I don't know why. yes / no

   Welcome! You will have a good time learning lots of new information.

Want to Learn More?

Recommended Reading

- *Pro-Life Answers to Pro-Choice Arguments* by Randy Alcorn
- *The Emerging Brave New World* by Thomas Glessner
- *Abortion Rites* by Marvin Olasky
- *Answering the Call* by John Ensor
- *Abortion and the Early Church* by Michael Gorman
- *Forced Exit* by Wesley Smith
- *How Should We Then Live?* by Frances Schaefer
- *Imbeciles* by Adam Cohen

Bibliography

Abortion Control Act. http://www.legis.state.pa.us/cfdocs/legis/LI/consCheck.cfm?txtType=HTM&ttl=18&div=0&chpt=32

Abortion Pill Reversal. http://abortionpillreversal.com/

Alcorn, Randy. *Pro-life Answers to Pro-choice Arguments*. Oregon: Multnomah Publishers, 2000.

Benatar, David. *Better Never to Have Been: The Harm of Coming Into Existence*. Oxford: Clarendon Press, 2006

Bilger, Micaiah. "Women are Dying From Legalized Abortions, But the Mainstream Media Will Never Tell You About It." Posted January 22, 2016. Life News. http://www.lifenews.com/2016/01/22/women-are-dying-form-legalized-abortions-but-the-mainstream-media-will-never-tell-you-about-it/

Black, Edwin. "The Horrifying American Roots of Nazi Eugenics." The George Washington University. Posted September 2003. http://historynewsnetwork.org/article/1796

Buck v. Bell. Legal Information Institute. (n.d.) https://www.law.cornell.edu/supremecourt/text/274/200

CBS News. "A Look Back, the Terri Schiavo Case." https://www.cbsnews.com/pictures/look-back-in-history-terri-schiavo-death/

Chapman, Michael. "NYC: More Black Babies Aborted Than Born." Posted February 20, 2014. CNS News Online. https://www.cnsnews.com/news/article/michael-w-chapman/nyc-more-black-babies-killed-abortion-born

Cohen, Adam. *Imbeciles: The Supreme Court, American Eugenics, and the Sterilization of Carrie Buck*. New York: Penguin Books, 2016.

Compelling Truth. "Who Was the Canaanite God Molech?" (n.d.) https://www.compellingtruth.org/molech.html

Cryer, Dan. "Shining Light on the Infamous Supreme Court Case and History of Eugenics in the US." Posted March 16, 2016. Boston Globe. https://www.bostonglobe.com/arts/2016/03/16/shining-light-infamous-supreme-court-case-and-history-eugenics/uf35rL8luWlHbEevARbJHP/story.html

Daar, Judith. *The New Eugenics: Selective Breeding in an Era of Reproductive Technologies.* London: Yale University Press, 2017.

Davis, Thomas N. III., M.D. *No Final Exit: A Psychiatrist's Rebuttal—Guidance for True Deliverance and Renewed Life.* Fletcher, North Carolina: New Puritan Library, 1992.

Dublin Declaration on Maternal Healthcare. https://www.dublindeclaration.com/

Dugdale, R.L. *The Jukes: A Study in Crime, Pauperism, Disease, and Heredity.* New York: G.P. Putnam's Sons, 1877.

Ensor, John. *Answering the Call: Saving Innocent Lives One Woman at a Time.* Peabody, Massachusetts: Hendrickson Publishing, 2012.

Eugenicsarchive.org "German/Nazi Eugenics." http://www.eugenicsarchive.org/eugenics/topics_fs.pl?theme=41

Eugenicsarchive.org "Buck vs. Bell." http://www.eugenicsarchive.org/html/eugenics/static/themes/39.html

Franks, Angela. *Margaret Sanger's Eugenic Legacy: The Control of Female Fertility.* London: McFarland and Company, 1971.

Gendercide definition. http://invisiblegirlproject.org/the-issue/

Glessner, Thomas. *The Emerging Brave New World.* HighWay, a division of Anomalos Publishing, 2008. *Created Equal: Reflections on the Unalienable Right to Life.* New York: Page Publishing, 2016.

Gorman, Michael J. *Abortion and the Early Church: Christian, Jewish, and Pagan Attitudes in the Greco-Roman World.* Illinois: Intervarsity Press, 1982.

Gosbell, Louise. ""As Long as It's Healthy": What Can We Learn from Early Christianity's Resistance to Infanticide and Exposure?" Posted March 13, 2019. ABC Religion and Ethics. https://www.abc.net.au/religion/early-christianitys-resistance-to-infanticide-and-exposure/10898016

Gould, J. *Your Death Warrant? The Implications of Euthanasia.* New Rochelle, NY: Arlington House, 1971.

Gudorf, Christine E. "Contraception and Abortion in Roman Catholicism." In Daniel C. Maguire (Ed.), *Sacred Rights: A Case for Contraceptives and Abortion in World Religions.* Oxford: Oxford University Press, 2003.

The Guttmacher Institute. *An Overview of Abortion Laws.* Posted May 1, 2019. https://www.guttmacher.org/state-policy/explore/overview-abortion-laws

Guyer, Michael. *Being Well-Born: An Introduction to Heredity and Eugenics* (2nd ed.). Indianapolis: The Bobbs-Merrill Company, 1927.

Handrick, Laura. "20 Best SMART Goals Examples for Small Businesses in 2018." Posted May 17, 2018. Fit Small Business. https://fitsmallbusiness.com/smart-goals-examples/

Heritage House. *Euthanasia: Mercy or Murder?* 2010, brochure.

Hill, Alexander. *Just Business: Christian Ethics for the Marketplace.* Downers Grove, Illinois: IVP Academic, 2018.

Hitler, Adolf. *Mein Kampf.* Boston: Houghton Mifflin, 1943. Pittsburgh University. http://www.pitt.edu/~syd/hit.html

Hull, N. E. H., & Hoffer, Peter Charles. *Roe v. Wade: The Abortion Rights Controversy in American History.* Lawrence, Kansas: University Press of Kansas, 2010.

Human Life Alliance. *Imposed Death, Euthanasia and Assisted Suicide.* https://resources.humanlife.org/pdf/imposed-death.pdf "Fact Sheets." https://resources.humanlife.org/?item_type=Fact-Sheet

Human Life International. "Exceptions: Is Abortion Ever Permissible?" 2015. https://www.hli.org/resources/exceptions-is-abortion-ever-permissible-2/

Humphry, Derek. *Final Exit.* Oregon: The Hemlock Society, 1991.

Huntington, E., Lorimer, F., & American Eugenics Society. *Tomorrow's Children: The Goal of Eugenics.* New York: J. Wiley & Sons, 1935.

Jaslow, Ryan. "Abortion Tied to Sharp Decline in Women's Mental Health." Posted September 1, 2011. CBS News. https://www.cbsnews.com/news/abortion-tied-to-sharp-decline-in-womens-mental-health/

Johnson, Abby. "The Dangerous Side of Birth Control." http://www.abbyjohnson.org/contraception

Kengor, Paul. *Abortion Racism in Pennsylvania: Where Abortion Wears a White Hood.* Posted May 12, 2019. The American Spectator. https://spectator.org/abortion-racism-in-pennsylvania/

Kiessling, Rebecca. "Rebecca's Story." https://rebeccakiessling.com/rebeccas-story/

Klusendorf, Scott. "What Are Bad Ways to Argue? A Review." Life Training Institute. https://prolifetraining.com/resources/the-case-for-life/#tab7

Kohl, Marvin. *Beneficent Euthanasia*. Buffalo: Prometheus Books, 1975.

Koskenniemi, E. *The Exposure of Infants among Jews and Christians in Antiquity*. Sheffield: Sheffield Phoenix Press, 2009. https://www.academia.edu/3600907/The_Exposure_of_Infants_among_Jews_and_Christians_in_Antiquity._The_Social_World_of_Biblical_Antiquity_Second_Series_4._Sheffield_Sheffield_Phoenix_Press_2009

Lahl, Jennifer. "Thank God Hippocrates Was Pagan." Posted August 1, 2012. The Center for Bioethics and Culture Network. http://www.cbc-network.org/2012/08/thank-god-hippocrates-was-pagan/

Lifton, Robert Jay. *The Nazi Doctors: Medical Killing and the Psychology of Genocide*. New York: Basic Books, 1986.

Live Action. "Margaret Sanger Quotes, History, and Biography." https://www.liveaction.org/research/margaret-sanger-quotes-history-and-biography

Lombardo, Paul. "Eugenic Sterilization Laws." Eugenics Archive. http://www.eugenicsarchive.org/html/eugenics/essay8text.html

Maguire, David. *The Unauthorized Guide to Sex and the Church*. Nashville: W Publishing Group, 2005.

Malthus, Thomas. *An Essay on the Principle of Overpopulation*. Oxford, Oxford University Press, 1999 (original in 1798).

Margaret Sanger Papers Project. "Birth Control or Race Control? Sanger and the Negro Project." New York University. Newsletter #28 (Fall 2001). https://www.nyu.edu/projects/sanger/articles/bc_or_race_control.php

Mattes, Brad. "Study Proves Abortion is More Dangerous than Childbirth." Posted September 12, 2014. Life News. http://www.lifenews.com/2014/09/12/study-proves-abortion-is-more-dangerous-than-childbirth/

Muers, Rachel. "Idolatry and Future Generations: The Persistence of Molech." *Modern Theology* 19, issue 4 (October 2003): 547-561 https://onlinelibrary.wiley.com/doi/abs/10.1111/1468-0025.00236

National Right to Life. "Quick Facts on RU486." https://www.nrlc.org/abortion/ru486/

Offit, P. A., & Tremblay, G. *Pandora's Lab: Seven Stories of Science Gone Wrong*. National Geographic, 2017.

Olasky, Marvin. *Abortion Rites: A Social History of Abortion in America*. Wheaton, Illinois: Crossway Books, 1992.

Olsen, Kirstin. *Chronology of Women's History*. Westport, Connecticut: Greenwood Press, 1994.

PAProLife.org. "Fact Sheets." https://www.paprolife.org/fact-sheets/"PA Abortion Law." https://www.paprolife.org/pa-abortion-law

Parke, Caleb, Gregg Re. "Dems Block "Born Alive" Bill to Provide Medical Care to Infants Who Survive Failed Abortions." Posted February 25, 2019. Fox News. https://www.foxnews.com/politics/senate-to-vote-on-born-alive-bill-to-protect-infants-who-survive-a-failed-abortion

Prioreschi, P. "The Hippocratic Oath: A Code for Physicians, Not a Pythagorean Manifesto." *Medical Hypotheses* (June 1995), 447–462. https://www.ncbi.nlm.nih.gov/pubmed/7476588

Pro-Life Action League. "Rape Abortion." https://prolifeaction.org/wp-content/uploads/docs/RapeAbortion.pdf

Radiance Foundation. "Just the Facts." http://www.theradiancefoundation.org/justthefacts/# "Ryan." http://radiancefoundation.org/ryan/

Reagan, Leslie J. *When Abortion Was a Crime: Women, Medicine, and Law in the United States, 1867-1973*. Berkeley, California: University of California Press, 2008.

Rehwinkel, Alfred Martin. *Planned Parenthood and Birth Control in the Light of Christian Ethics*. Saint Louis: Concordia Publishing, 1959.

Religious Coalition for Reproductive Choice. "Mission Statement." http://rcrc.org/mission-statement/

Roe v. Wade. Legal Information Institute (n.d.) https://www.law.cornell.edu/supremecourt/text/410/113

Sanger, Margaret. *Margaret Sanger: An Autobiography*. New York: W.W. Norton, 1938. "A Letter from Margaret Sanger to Dr. C.J. Gamble." 1939. http://genius.com/2657260 *The Pivot of Civilization*. 1922. http://www.gutenberg.org/ebooks/1689?msg=welcome_stranger#link2HCH0005

Schaeffer, Francis A. *How Should We Then Live?* New Jersey: Fleming H. Revell Company, 1976. *Whatever Happened to the Human Race?* New Jersey: Fleming H. Revell Company, 1979.

Scott, Emmet. "The Role of Infanticide and Abortion in Pagan Rome's Decline." *New English Review* (October 2012). http://newenglishreview.org/custpage.cfm/frm/123665/sec_id/123665

Secular Pro-Life. "Our Mission." http://www.secularprolife.org/mission

Sider, Ronald J. *The Early Church on Killing: A Comprehensive Sourcebook on War, Abortion, and Capital Punishment.* Grand Rapids, Michigan: Baker Academic, 2012.

Silent No More Awareness Campaign. http://www.silentnomoreawareness.org/

Smith, L., & Coloma, C. *Renting Lacy: A Story of America's Prostituted Children.* Arlington, Virginia: Shared Hope International, 2013.

Smith, Wesley J. *Forced Exit: Euthanasia, Assisted Suicide, and the New Duty to Die.* New York: Encounter Books, 1997.

Stangl, R. "Selective Terminations and Respect for the Disabled." *Journal of Medicine & Philosophy* 35, no.1 (February 2010), 32-45.

Stenzel, Pam. http://www.pamstenzel.com/

Stone, Geoffrey R. *Sex and the Constitution: Sex, Religion, and Law from America's Origins to the Twenty-First Century.* New York: Liveright Publishing, 2017.

TooManyAborted.org. "The Negro Project." http://www.toomanyaborted.com/thenegroproject/

V, Lynn. "What 1,000 Abortions Have Taught Me." Feminist Women's Health Center. 1993. http://www.fwhc.org/abortion/1000ab.htm

Wallace, W. R. "The Hand That Rocks the Cradle is the Hand That Rules the World." http://www.potw.org/archive/potw391.html

Washington Post. "Suicide Note Said to Accuse Author." (n.d.). https://www.washingtonpost.com/archive/lifestyle/1991/10/28/suicide-note-said-to-accuse-author/f1bcba4e-7cf1-4530-a17f-101523609f60/?noredirect=on&utm_term=.5b263454396f

Yarmohammadi, Hassan, et al. "An Investigation into the Ancient Abortion Laws: Comparing Ancient Persia with Ancient Greece and Rome." *Acta Medico-historica Adriatica* 11, no. 2 (January 2013), 291–298.

Zoloth, Laurie. "Each One an Entire World: A Jewish Perspective on Family Planning" in Daniel C. Maguire (ed.), *Sacred Texts: A Case for Contraceptives and Abortion in World Religions*. Oxford: Oxford University Press, 2003.

ENDNOTES

1. Yarmohammadi, H. "An Investigation into the Ancient Abortion Laws: Comparing Ancient Persia with Ancient Greece and Rome." *Acta Medico-historica Adriatica*, January 2013.
2. Yarmohammadi, H. "An Investigation into the Ancient Abortion Laws: Comparing Ancient Persia with Ancient Greece and Rome."
3. Glessner, T. *The Emerging Brave New World*. HighWay Publishing, 2008, p. 18.
4. Glessner, T. *The Emerging Brave New World*, p. 18.
5. Prioreschi, P. "The Hippocratic Oath: A Code for Physicians not a Pythagorean Manifesto." *Medical Hypotheses*, June 1995.
6. Prioreschi, P. "The Hippocratic Oath: A Code for Physicians not a Pythagorean Manifesto."
7. Glessner, T. *The Emerging Brave New World*, p. 18.
8. Yarmohammadi, H. "An Investigation into the Ancient Abortion Laws: Comparing Ancient Persia with Ancient Greece and Rome."
9. Glessner, T. *The Emerging Brave New World*, p. 19.
10. Gendercide definition. Invisiblegirlproject.org/the-issue/
11. Gorman, M. *Abortion and the Early Church*. Intervarsity Press, 1982, p. 14.
12. Gorman, M. *Abortion and the Early Church*, p. 22.
13. Gorman, M. *Abortion and the Early Church*, p. 20.
14. Olsen, K. *Chronology of Women's History*. Greenwood Press, 1994, p. 18.
15. Gorman, M. *Abortion and the Early Church*, p. 21.
16. Gorman, M. *Abortion and the Early Church*, p. 15.
17. Scott, E. "The Role of Infanticide and Abortion in Pagan Rome's Decline." *New English Review*, October 2012.
18. Scott, E. "The Role of Infanticide and Abortion in Pagan Rome's Decline."
19. Gorman, M. *Abortion and the Early Church*, p. 43.
20. Gorman, M. *Abortion and the Early Church*, p. 48.
21. Gorman, M. *Abortion and the Early Church*, p. 48.
22. Sider, R. *The Early Church on Killing: A Comprehensive Sourcebook on War, Abortion, and Capital Punishment*. Baker Academic, 2012, p. 19.
23. Sider, R. *The Early Church on Killing*, p. 20.
24. Gorman, M. *Abortion and the Early Church*, p. 55.
25. Sider, R. *The Early Church on Killing*, p. 115.
26. Gorman, M. *Abortion and the Early Church*, p. 70.
27. Gorman, M. *Abortion and the Early Church*, pgs. 70-73.
28. Gorman, M. *Abortion and the Early Church*, p. 42.
29. Gosbell, L. ""As Long as It's Healthy": What Can We Learn from Early Christianity's Resistance to Infanticide and Exposure?" ABC Religion and Ethics.
30. Olasky, M. *Abortion Rites: A Social History of Abortion in America*. Crossway Books, 1992, p. 20.
31. Olasky, M. *Abortion Rites*, p. 29.
32. Olasky, M. *Abortion Rites*, p. 29.
33. Olasky, M. *Abortion Rites*, p. 31.
34. Olasky, M. *Abortion Rites*, p. 30.
35. Olasky, M. *Abortion Rites*, p. 33.
36. Olasky, M. *Abortion Rites*, ch. 1; Hull, N. *Roe v. Wade: The Abortion Rights Controversy in American History*. University Press of Kansas, 2010, ch. 1.
37. Olasky, M. *Abortion Rites*, p. 38.

38. Olasky, M. *Abortion Rites*, p. 48.
39. Olasky, M. *Abortion Rites*, p. 178.
40. Olasky, M. *Abortion Rites*, ch. 1.
41. Hull, N. *Roe v. Wade: The Abortion Rights Controversy in American History*, p. 20
42. Hull, N. *Roe v. Wade: The Abortion Rights Controversy in American History*, p. 21.
43. Olasky, M. *Abortion Rites*, p. 61.
44. Hull, N. *Roe v. Wade: The Abortion Rights Controversy in American History*, p. 26.
45. Olasky, M. *Abortion Rites*, p. 63.
46. Olasky, M. *Abortion Rites*, p. 64.
47. Hull, N. *Roe v. Wade: The Abortion Rights Controversy in American History*, p. 28.
48. Olasky, M. *Abortion Rites*, p. 163.
49. Stone, G. *Sex and the Constitution: Sex, Religion, and Law from America's Origins to the Twenty-First Century*. Liveright Publishing, 2017, p. 186
50. Olasky, M. *Abortion Rites*, p. 137.
51. Olasky, M. *Abortion Rites*, p. 180.
52. Olasky, M. *Abortion Rites*, ch. 9.
53. Olasky, M. *Abortion Rites*, p. 215.
54. Olasky, M. *Abortion Rites*, ch. 9.
55. Olasky, M. *Abortion Rites*, p. 228.
56. Olasky, M. *Abortion Rites*, p. 248.
57. Olasky, M. *Abortion Rites*, p. 250.
58. Olasky, M. *Abortion Rites*, p. 274.
59. Olasky, M. *Abortion Rites*, p. 276.
60. Stone, G. *Sex and the Constitution*, p. 370.
61. Rehwinkel, A. *Planned Parenthood and Birth Control in the Light of Christian Ethics*. Concordia Publishing, 1959, p. 25.
62. Stone, G. *Sex and the Constitution*, p. 389.
63. Parke, C. "Dems Block "Born Alive" Bill to Provide Medical Care to Infants Who Survive Failed Abortions." Fox News, 2019.
64. Reagan, L. *When Abortion Was a Crime: Women, Medicine, and Law in the United States*. University of California Press, 2008, p. 47; Olasky, M. *Abortion Rites*, pgs. 152-161.
65. Olasky, M. *Abortion Rites*, p. 154.
66. Glessner, T. *Created Equal: Reflections on the Unalienable Right to Life*. Page Publishing, 2016, p. 158.
67. Glessner, T. *Created Equal*, p. 165.
68. Roe v. Wade. Legal Information Institute.
69. Stone, G. *Sex and the Constitution*, p. 398.
70. Stone, G. *Sex and the Constitution*, p. 398.
71. National Right to Life. "Quick Facts on RU486."
72. Abortion Pill Reversal.
73. Huntington, E. *Tomorrow's Children: The Goal of Eugenics*. Wiley & Sons, 1935, p. viii.
74. Offit, P. *Pandora's Lab: Seven Stories of Science Gone Wrong*. National Geographic, 2017, p. 102.
75. Guyer, M. *Being Well-Born: An Introduction to Heredity and Eugenics*. Bobbs-Merril Company, 1927, p. 414.
76. Cohen, A. *Imbeciles: The Supreme Court, American Eugenics, and the Sterilization of Carrie Buck*. Penguin Books, 2016, p. 45.
77. Cohen, A. *Imbeciles*, p. 45.
78. Lombardo, P. Eugenic Sterilization Laws.
79. Huntington, E. *Tomorrow's Children*, p. 5-6.
80. Huntington, E. *Tomorrow's Children*, p. 17.
81. Huntington, E. *Tomorrow's Children*, p. 16.
82. Cohen, A. *Imbeciles*, p. 145.

83. Huntington, E. *Tomorrow's Children*, p. 52.
84. Buck v. Bell. Legal Information Institute.
85. Sanger, M. *The Pivot of Civilization*, 1922, ch. 5.
86. Live Action. "Margaret Sanger Quotes, History, and Biography."
87. Hitler, A. *Mein Kampf*. 1943.
88. Offit, P. *Pandora's Lab*, p. 105.
89. Chapman, M. "NYC: More Black Babies Aborted Than Born." CNS News, 2014.
90. Radiance Foundation. "Just the Facts."
91. National Right to Life. "Birth Control or Race Control? Sanger and the Negro Project." NY University, 2001.
92. Sanger, Margaret. "A Letter from Margaret Sanger to Dr. C.J. Gamble." 1939.
93. Kengor, P. *Abortion Racism in Pennsylvania. Where Abortion Wears a White Hood*. The American Spectator, 2019.
94. Humphry, Derek. *Final Exit*. The Hemlock Society, 1991, p. 20.
95. Humphry, Derek. *Final Exit*, p. 66.
96. Heritage House. "Euthanasia: Mercy or Murder?" 2010.
97. Heritage House. "Euthanasia: Mercy or Murder?"
98. Heritage House. "Euthanasia: Mercy or Murder?"
99. Heritage House. "Euthanasia: Mercy or Murder?"
100. Humphry, Derek. Final Exit, p. 17.
101. Washington Post. "Suicide Note Said to Accuse Author."
102. Smith, W. *Forced Exit: Euthanasia, Assisted Suicide, and the New Duty to Die*. Encounter Books, 1997, p. 15.
103. Paprolife.org. Fact Sheets.
104. CBS News. "A Look Back, the Terri Schiavo Case."
105. Human Life Alliance. *Imposed Death: Euthanasia and Assisted Suicide*.
106. Humphry, Derek. *Final Exit*, p. 75.
107. Humphry, Derek. *Final Exit*, ch. 7.
108. Smith, W. *Forced Exit*, p. 88.
109. Secular Pro-Life. Our Mission.
110. Religious Coalition for Reproductive Choice. Mission Statement.
111. Silent No More Awareness Campaign.
112. V, Lynn. "What 1,000 Abortions Have Taught Me." Feminist Women's Health Center, 1993.
113. Bilger, M. "Women are Dying From Legalized Abortions, But the Mainstream Media Will Never Tell You About It." Life News, 2016.
114. Mattes, B. "Study Proves Abortion is More Dangerous than Childbirth." Life News, 2014.
115. Pro-Life Action League. "Rape Abortion."
116. Human Life International. "Exceptions: Is Abortion Ever Permissible?" 2015.
117. Klusendorf, S. "What are Bad Ways to Argue? A Review." Life Training Institute.
118. Kiessling, R. "Rebecca's Story."
119. Radiance Foundation. "Ryan."
120. Stenzel, Pam.
121. Dublin Declaration on Maternal Healthcare.
122. Handrick, L. "20 Best SMART Goals Examples for Small Businesses in 2018." Fit Small Business.
123. Nahum 1:14; 3:19; Zephaniah 2:13-15; Is.10:5-19
124. Jaslow, R. "Abortion Tied to a Sharp Decline in Women's Mental Health." CBS News, 2011.
125. Wallace, W. "The Hand That Rocks the Cradle is the Hand That Rules the World."
126. The Guttmacher Institute. "An Overview of Abortion Laws." 2019.